SHRUBS &
DECORATIVE
EVERGREENS

PUBLISHER'S NOTE

As an English horticulturist now working in America I can heartily recommend this series of gardening books. In them you will find a wealth of sound principles and practical ideas, equally applicable in the U.S.A. and Great Britain.

As you read this book bear in mind that individual cultivars recommended for specific purposes may not be available throughout the U.S.A. and similar kinds will have to be sought to achieve the same effect. Also, because of the vast climatic differences within the U.S., some of the guidelines regarding planting in sun or shade may have to be modified. Be sure to consider local conditions when deciding whether or not a particular plant will be hardy in your garden as many regions of the U.S. experience winters far more severe than those in the British Isles.

Most recommendations for fertilizers, weed and pest control refer to their active ingredients. Commercial sources have been avoided, enabling the reader to identify a local product suitable for the job in hand.

The application of common names to plants can vary. Therefore, it is not surprising to find a few names that may not be recognized by all readers, such as 'Busy Lizzie' (Impatiens) and 'Mind Your Own Business' (Baby Tears). Such names are very few and readers will have no difficulty in relating to specific plant descriptions and cultivation techniques. A glossary is included to define the few words and phrases that may not be familiar.

David Mason

Manager, Sassafras Nursery
Topanga, California

SHRUBS &
DECORATIVE
EVERGREENS

Alan Toogood

GALLERY BOOKS
An Imprint of W. H. Smith Publishers Inc.
112 Madison Avenue
New York City 10016

ACKNOWLEDGEMENTS

The publishers gratefully acknowledge the following agencies for granting permission to reproduce the colour photographs: Harry Smith Horticultural Photographic Collection (pp. 4, 26, 30, 47, 51, 54, 55, 67, 72, 83 and 91) and Pat Brindley (pp. 10, 58, 62 and 71).

All the line drawings are by Nils Solberg.

© Ward Lock Limited 1988, 1990

First published in Great Britain in 1988
by Ward Lock Limited, Artillery House,
Artillery Row, London SW1P 1RT, a Cassell Company.

This edition published in 1990 by Gallery Books,
an imprint of W.H. Smith Publishers, Inc., 112
Madison Avenue, New York, New York 10016.

Gallery Books are available for bulk purchase for
sales promotions and premium use. For details write
or telephone the Manager of Special Sales, W.H. Smith
Publishers, Inc., 112 Madison Avenue, New York, New
York 10016. (212) 532-6600.

Text filmset in Bembo
by Hourds Typographica, Stafford
Printed in Portugal

ISBN 0-8317-7174-7

Front cover: Rhododendron and *Clematis macropetala*, courtesy Harry Smith Horticultural Photographic Collection.

Frontispiece: Many shrubs are noted for their colourful foliage such as variegated, purple, gold and grey and these can be combined to create some stunning contrasts in colour and texture.

CONTENTS

PREFACE

Of all the groups of plants available today shrubs represent particularly good value for money as most are very long-lived. Indeed, some of them can last a lifetime.

A collection of shrubs can provide colour and interest all the year round, from flowers, foliage, berries and coloured bark. Above all, and most important for many people in this busy modern world, the majority of shrubs are very labour-saving, particularly the ground-cover kinds, needing little or no attention once established.

In modern garden design shrubs, being permanent and woody in nature, generally form the main "framework" of a bed or border. Between and around them other plants, like hardy perennials, bulbs and annuals, are grown for contrast and additional interest. Hence the "mixed border" – a feature of most modern gardens.

There is a vast range of shrubs available, which can be confusing to the beginner. So the purpose of this book is to make choosing shrubs as easy as possible. Only really garden-worthy kinds have been included and you will find the very best of the newest varieties.

This book helps you choose suitable shrubs for your soil and climate and gives plenty of advice on growing them really well. Soil preparation and planting techniques are covered, as are aspects of care like pruning – although by no means all shrubs need pruning. Most people like to try their hand at propagation and so the best technique is given for each shrub described.

With the aid of the comprehensive, detailed descriptive lists and the beautiful colour photographs you will have no trouble in choosing a collection of shrubs for your garden – indeed, the problem will be what not to buy!

A.T.

GLOSSARY

Chalk soils	soils with a high level of akalinity
Dibber	a blunt, pencil-like instrument used to make holes for inserting seedlings
Hessian/sacking	burlap
Pricking out	transplanting young seedlings

CHAPTER I

IN PRAISE OF SHRUBS

A shrub is usually defined as a woody perennial that branches from or just above ground level. It differs from a herbaceous perennial in that it does not die down to ground level each winter but builds up a permanent framework of branches with every passing season. So, of course, does a tree, which is also a woody perennial, but a tree differs from a shrub in that it is usually defined as having an unbranched stem for at least 1.8 m (6 ft) above the ground.

Such a succinct definition does not, however, give the slightest idea of the range of plants. There are, to begin with, some 5,900 woody perennials that can be grown out of doors in the British Isles. Of those some 800 are highly ornamental and, in the main, easily grown shrubs which can readily be obtained from garden centres and nurseries. Yet even this limited number of shrubs provides a variety of shapes (including leaf shapes), flower, foliage and bark colour and seasons of interest. Furthermore, once properly planted in soil that has been well prepared to suit their needs, they will become a permanent asset to the garden, needing little attention once established and increasing in size and beauty with each passing year.

To many people the greatest virtue of shrubs is that they are (in the main) inexpensive to buy and in terms of the ground they cover and the contribution they make to the garden as a whole, are the finest investment in the plant kingdom. And this is true: no other group of plants will give such a rewarding return on capital laid out; nor will any other group do this over so many years, or with so little effort.

Many other people consider their greatest virtue is smothering the weeds that grow under them and, again, this is completely true: a great many will do just that, especially evergreens. Care must be taken in the selection of shrubs, though, for not all of them will do this.

Yet to anyone who is looking at the garden not so much with a view simply to finding the most economic and least demanding occupants for a patch of bare ground, but rather with a view to creating a three-dimensional picture of lasting but eternally changing beauty, the sheer diversity of shrubs is their greatest virtue.

To many inexperienced gardeners a shrub is just a bushy thing with leaves and flowers. There is infinitely more to shrubs than this. There are little creeping shrubs that crawl along the ground, growing no more than a couple of inches high, and shrubs which, though slow-growing, ultimately reach the dimensions of a small tree. There are shrubs that grow upright, like a guardsman on parade, and others that spread themselves leisurely over the ground, leaning on it here and there and rooting as they go. Many form really bushy specimens, others may weep or form mushroom-shaped or pyramidal bushes. Some stand with their 'arms' outstretched like scarecrows: some are as graceful in growth as a ballerina, while others are as rugged and gnarled as the olives in the Mediterranean. Some form wood hard enough to blunt even the sharpest pruning saw and others, like the tree paeonies, *Paeonia suffruticosa,* or the Californian tree poppy, *Romneya coulteri,* are only semi-shrubby, about half of each year's growth dying back to the half that has ripened.

Probably the first thing the inexperienced gardener wants to know about a shrub is whether it has huge flowers. Certainly many do. Probably the largest flowers to be found on any shrub are those borne by the tree paeonies, *Paeonia suffruticosa*, which can measure as much as 45 cm (18 in) across and come in every shade from purest white to scarlets and crimsons, with every conceivable shade of pink in between. The flowers can further vary by being single, semi-double or very double. The fact that they are huge may not necessarily make them good garden plants: the flowers of some tree paeonies are so heavy that they simply hang their faces unless one props them up. The smaller-flowered forms are usually better garden plants. But there are other plants that have very large flowers, notably the magnolias, especially *Magnolia liliiflora* 'Nigra', which has huge chalice-shaped flowers, or the paler pinkish-purple *M.* × *soulangiana*, which flowers in spring on bare branches before the leaves appear. The tree poppies, *Romneya coulteri* and *R.* × *hybrida*, also have huge flowers, 15 cm (6 in) or more across.

The size of the individual flowers is not by any means the only criterion by which to judge the merit of a shrub. Lilacs, for example, have individually small flowers, but these are borne in huge numbers in densely packed spikes and the spike as a whole may be just as effective, perhaps even more so, than an individual flower of the same size. In the spiraeas the flowers are relatively small but, again, produced in dense clusters, creating a far more effective inflorescence than the size of the individual flower would lead one to expect. Other shrubs, like *Cotinus coggygria* and the tamarisks, present their flowers in very loose sprays, often of a very open and airy nature, and yet borne in such abundance as to be highly effective.

The leaves of shrubs can vary, too (Fig. 1). They may be elliptic,

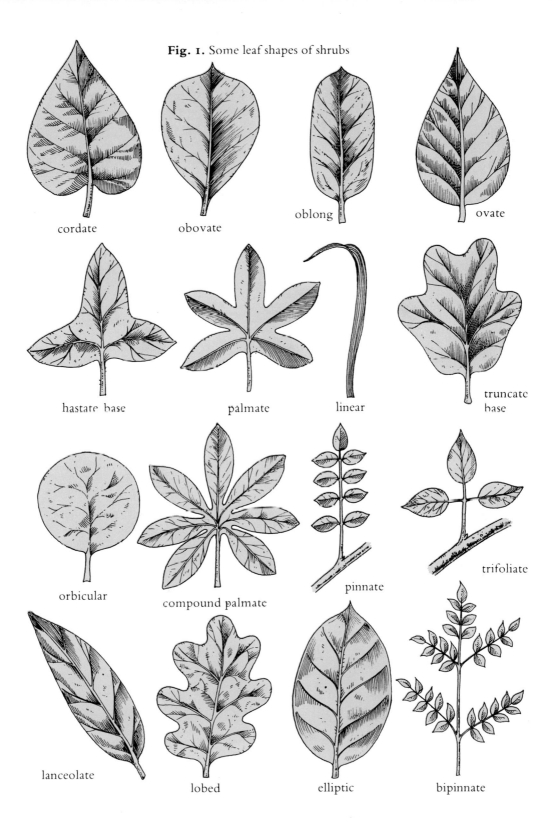

Fig. 1. Some leaf shapes of shrubs

cordate

obovate

oblong

ovate

hastate base

palmate

linear

truncate base

orbicular

compound palmate

pinnate

trifoliate

lanceolate

lobed

elliptic

bipinnate

The tree poppy, *Romneya coulteri*, produces its fragrant blooms from mid-summer to mid-autumn if given a very sunny spot.

palmate, pinnate, bipinnate, lanceolate, ovate, oblong, obovate, trifoliate, hastate, lobed, linear and many other shapes. But that is only a beginning. They can be any of these shapes, but large or small. And, though most people tend to think of shrubs as having green leaves, they can be many other colours as well. Even in green there is enormous variation: the leaves of laurel and some rhododendrons and camellias are very dark black-green: while the leaves of *Pittosporum tenuifolium* are light silvery green and those of some of the magnolias a bright, fresh green. Some shrubs have bronze, purple or copper leaves, while others have variegated leaves, margined, blotched or splashed with cream, yellow, white or pink.

The majority of shrubs produce seed heads and a similar range of variation may be found among these. Most shrubs have rather dull seed heads, like those of lilacs or escallonias, yet some are more spectacular. The smoke bush, *Cotinus coggygria,* retains its delicate plumes long after they have finished flowering, imperceptibly changing from flowers to seedheads, yet remaining beautiful all the time. Other shrubs like the cotoneasters are grown for their colourful berries. These are usually red or orange but there are shrubs like *Callicarpa bodinieri giraldii* in which the berries are an unexpected bright violet and *Symplocos paniculata* in which they are brilliant turquoise.

The bark of shrubs can vary just as much and a number of willows and dogwoods are grown solely for the brilliant colouring (usually bright red or bright yellow) of their young twigs in winter. They need to be pruned hard each spring for these bark effects to be seen at their best.

Then there is the shrubs' flowering season. The season starts with the witch hazels, notably *Hamamelis mollis,* which flowers in mid-winter if the weather is mild, its spidery yellow blossoms giving the air around the shrub a rich scent. This is followed by the wintersweet, *Chimonanthus praecox,* and that, a little later, by *Cornus mas* in late winter/early spring. As the year goes on the number of shrubs in flower increases until early summer, a period which probably has more shrubs in flower than any other time of the year. After that the number in flower diminishes again.

From the gardener's point of view the ideal shrub would be one which had an attractive habit of growth, variegated foliage, good flowers followed by attractive autumn leaf colouring and then by brightly coloured fruits with, for good measure, good bark colour in the dead of winter. Unfortunately there is no shrub which measures up to this impossible ideal. So to achieve all these effects one has to select a number of different shrubs, each of which contributes one or more of these qualities to the group planting.

CHAPTER 2

MAKING THE MOST OF SHRUBS

Such is the diversity of shrubs that a garden can be planted with them and virtually nothing else and still be a joy through every week of the year – though the garden will achieve a richer texture if herbaceous plants and spring and autumn flowering bulbs are also used, some of which could perhaps be planted in the lawn to add another dimension to the garden.

The term 'shrubbery' is rather outmoded now and carries connotations of rather gloomy Victorian plantings of deadly dull evergreens, especially aucubas and privets, which are still to be seen (to their eternal disgrace) in many public parks. Yet perhaps it is precisely because of these extremely dull plantings that pure 'shrubberies' passed out of fashion and the 'mixed border' (i.e. a border containing a mixture of both herbaceous and shrubby material) came to replace it. In all fairness to the Victorians, it should be stressed that they simply did not have the range of colourful flowering and foliage shrubs that we have today. The majority of the most attractive shrubs that can be grown in gardens today have been collected since Victorian times.

Today there is such a wealth of good shrubs that anyone contemplating making a shrub garden is likely to finish up planting more than there is room for. This *embarras de richesses* means that one has to exercise some self-control in choosing plants, and to discipline one's imagination, especially while reading nurserymen's glowing descriptions of everything in their list. It is worth remembering that catalogues are produced to sell plants: each description of a plant is a mini-advertisement.

Shrubs probably constitute the most economic way of planting a garden. Many can be bought for little more than the cost of a box of bedding plants and once planted need little further care. They will increase in size and stature year by year and if planted the correct distance apart will join ranks and keep out weeds. Some, it is true, do better if pruned regularly, but for the busy gardener there are so many to choose from that never need pruning that even this chore can be omitted. Some shrubs are better at keeping down weeds than others and the chore of weeding can be minimized if only those shrubs which are really good ground-cover plants are selected. Yet even limitations like these embrace a sufficiently wide range of shrubs to make a really attractive garden.

The diversity of shrubs is so great that the real problem is not choosing what to include in one's garden but what to leave out. One can, if desired, have shrubs in flower every month of the year. In a small garden, one may then well find that there are only one or two in flower at any one time of the year. Or one may choose to have a great burst of colour in spring and early summer, with the garden rather less colourful later in the year – though if this is the option one goes for, it is worth remembering that roses are shrubs and will give colour from mid-summer until first frosts; and that if one leaves some beds aside for bedding plants these will be at their best once the early shrubs are over.

There is another way of looking at the problem of what to plant – discount flowers to begin with and try to create something with foliage colours, making the most of shrubs with coloured or variegated leaves. At the same time variation in texture of plants is worth aiming for.

When you have ensured there will be plenty of foliage colour and interesting textures from both deciduous and evergreen shrubs, you can start thinking about flowers and berries. Wherever possible choose shrubs which have a very long flowering period, or which hold on to their berries for several months. It is a sheer waste of space in a small garden to plant shrubs which have but fleeting floral beauty. Unfortunately this is true of some of our most popular shrubs like lilacs, mock orange and forsythia.

However, gardening is an art, not a science. It is not the individual plants that are important but the total effect created by combining them. You should aim for contrasts in colour, shape and size. To achieve this, try to select shrubs with both large and small flowers; large and small leaves; and either rounded, ferny or spiky foliage. You will need shrubs with grey, purple, golden and variegated foliage to contrast with those that have plain green leaves.

Other aspects should be considered too, like the habit of the shrub: thus, rather than growing only bushy shrubs it is worth including one or two that are of narrowly columnar habit and carry their branches erect. It is also worth contrasting these with shrubs of a weeping habit, the majority of these forming mushroom-shaped bushes. A large number of shrubs are more or less prostrate and most of these make excellent ground cover. They should be used with great freedom, not only at the front of the border but also under those shrubs which do not keep weeds down.

In painting the picture of one's shrub garden some care and thought should be given to mixing evergreens and deciduous plants. Though evergreens are generally (but not invariably) better at keeping down weeds than deciduous shrubs and it is tempting to plant more of them for that reason, if unrelieved by the inclusion of some deciduous shrubs they rapidly become monotonous unless care has been taken to include quite a high proportion of evergreens with variegated foliage, as well as plenty of contrast in foliage size and shape. Even then, the evergreens are always there, always the same, just increasing in size year by year and producing their often fine display of flowers, so they tend to become boring. The inclusion of deciduous shrubs adds a different dimension to the border: it immediately makes noticeable the changing of the seasons. The bare twigs may not necessarily be attractive in winter, but they pave the way for the eternal surprise of spring, with its fresh green foliage – something which passes almost unnoticed when the evergreens put on their new leaves. And then there is autumn colour, something which is naturally an impossibility among evergreens, though the leaves of a number of evergreens, including conifers, do change colour in winter. Evergreens also make the finest foil of all for autumn colour.

When it comes to using plants with variegated or coloured leaves again some care should be given to siting them. A variegated deciduous shrub can be planted anywhere: it will come into its own in its own season. But a variegated evergreen will be far more appreciated if planted where it passes almost unnoticed throughout the summer, only to come into its own in winter when its presence is suddenly revealed by the falling of the leaves of some deciduous shrub planted in front of it. Surprises of this sort help to keep the garden interesting throughout the year.

Opposite: Autumn colour. This is something shrubs can contribute to a garden just as well as trees. The plant shown here is *Cotinus coggygria.*

· CHAPTER 3 ·

CHOOSING AND BUYING SHRUBS

You should aim to choose shrubs that are well suited to your garden, taking into account the type of soil and the climate. Some shrubs are very adaptable but others have special needs, such as a lime-free soil, or a warm sheltered spot because they are on the tender side.

WHAT WILL GROW IN YOUR SOIL?

The first thing to find out about any garden is what will grow in the soil. Earth may just be earth to many of us, but plants are more fussy. Your soil may be clay or sandy, it may be peaty or chalky or a good rich crumbly loam. What will grow well on a dry sandy soil will often simply rot away on a heavy clay soil. These terms describe the texture of the soil, which can be changed in a number of ways, nearly always by adding more humus to it, though clay soils need coarse sand or grit added to improve drainage.

More important than the texture of your soil is whether it is acid, alkaline or neutral. This really is important. If it is acid you will be able to grow the lime-hating shrubs like rhododendrons, camellias, kalmias, heathers (although some of these will grow in chalky soils) and many other choice subjects. If your soil is alkaline (limy or chalky) you will not be able to grow any of these, but you still have an enormous variety of first-rate shrubs to choose from.

To find out whether your soil is acid or alkaline simply look around you. If there are rhododendrons in most of your neighbours' gardens, and if they look in good health, the chances are that you are on acid soil. If on the other hand there is not a rhododendron, camellia or heather to be seen for miles around, you are almost certainly living in an alkaline area. Weeds, too, can tell you quite a lot about your soil. If bracken, for example, is common in your area, that is a further indication that you are on acid soil.

A more accurate way of determining the acidity or alkalinity of your soil is to use a soil-testing kit. Most are inexpensive and easy to use. They can be bought from most garden centres. Just follow the simple instructions that come with the kit and in a short time you will have an accurate knowledge of the soil in your garden. Acidity or alkalinity is measured on the pH scale. A reading of pH7 means you have a neutral soil: a higher figure means it is alkaline, a lower figure that it is acid. When testing your soil it is worth taking readings from several parts of the garden: it is likely that the builders will have scattered rubble in some part of the garden and the soil there is likely to give a different reading from soil elsewhere.

If you are lucky enough to have an acid or neutral soil never add lime – you will regret it some day. It is worth remembering that most shrubs which grow well in alkaline conditions will also thrive in acid soils. Lime-hating shrubs will quickly die, though, if you plant them in limy or chalky soils.

WHAT WILL GROW IN YOUR CLIMATE?

Climate is the next major factor involved in deciding what will grow in your garden. Roughly speaking the further north you go in the British Isles the colder the climate: the winters become longer and harder, and the intensity of the sunlight in the summer is reduced. This means that the further north you live the hardier the shrubs you need to grow. The western half of the British Isles is also generally warmer but also wetter than the eastern half: this makes it ideal for growing broadleaved (as opposite to coniferous) evergreens. The eastern half is generally drier and sunnier and ideal for growing deciduous shrubs. The south-west provides the warmest, but also the dampest, climate in the British Isles, and that is where you will find the finest specimens of tender shrubs being grown. The north-east is the coldest, bleakest part of the country where anything that is not bone hardy has little chance of survival. Coastal areas are special cases, being relatively free from frost but suffering from destructive winds.

Over the British Isles as a whole wind is the greatest enemy of all. Unless you have some sort of shelter from winds, particularly from the cold northerlies and easterlies, many shrubs will never become established. If you are lucky enough to have a garden that is already sheltered by other gardens and established plants you will be able to grow a far wider range of shrubs than if your garden is on a bleak new estate. If that is the case you will have to provide some sort of wind protection such as an open-work fence or a hedge. A solid fence or wall gives little protection: in fact it causes turbulence, which can damage plants. The ideal fence is a semi-permeable one that lets about 50 per cent of the wind through, but filters it or breaks its force. Trelliswork screens clothed with climbing plants make excellent windbreaks.

The other limiting factor is frost, especially late-spring frost which can kill young growth: if this occurs year after year a shrub may never get any larger, may never flower and may in time die. Late spring frosts hit hardest in frost-pockets: valleys and sheltered hollows. Just as hot air rises, so frost sinks, always seeking the lowest point. If your garden is on a slope make sure there is a gap in the defences at the lowest part of the garden through which frost can drain away.

On the other hand, many of the most beautiful shrubs are tender. The uninitiated may view with great dismay the loss of such a shrub due to severe frost but the keen gardener will generally prefer to try it and be grateful if it survives a run of a few mild winters and then succumbs. Such gardeners feel it is better to have enjoyed a treasure for a few years than never to have grown it at all. Those who are not prepared to take such risks should plant only completely hardy shrubs.

FINDING OUT ABOUT SHRUBS

The catalogues of our well-known shrub specialists are mines of information. They give detailed descriptions of each plant, including size, and indicate any special needs such as soil and climate. Nevertheless, do try to see shrubs growing before you buy them: ideally mature specimens. Also make notes of pleasing combinations or groups of shrubs – there is no harm at all in copying other people's ideas! There are many places where you can see shrubs growing well. Many public and botanic gardens have vast collections of shrubs, all clearly labelled. To see them at their best it is probably better to go to those private gardens that are open to the public, either all the year round or at selected weekends throughout the year. You can find details of these in your local newspaper or from garden-visiting booklets. A great many National Trust properties maintain first-rate gardens. Many nurseries and garden centres also have collections of shrubs.

It is only when you see shrubs growing that you get any real idea of how they will look in your garden. And it is always worth carrying a note-pad and pencil to make a note of anything you have not come across before that you find really striking. Do, however, check on the habit of the plant. A large, imposing specimen may have taken years to reach that size; or it may take many years to settle down before it starts flowering. This is particularly true of many larger magnolias, for example. When you know about such habits disappointment can be avoided.

It is always interesting to visit flower shows, especially those of the Royal Horticultural Society, but the show bench can be misleading.

Shrubs and trees together combine to give a mellow texture to a garden, clothing it from the ground upwards.

What one often sees is a spray of bloom. This gives one no idea how the shrub grows or how profusely it flowers. It doesn't even give one an idea when the shrub flowers, for it may have been forced into flower for the show, or retarded by keeping it cool. And if you see an excellent display of berries bear in mind that they have probably been protected from birds by netting for several weeks, and that in your garden the birds might strip the lot in a week.

WHERE TO BUY

You can buy shrubs from a good local nursery or garden centre, or by mail-order from one of our specialist shrub nurserymen. You will have a far wider choice of plants and varieties if you choose from a specialist's catalogue. Most garden centres have a more limited selection and naturally stock only the most popular kinds which sell well. Although it should be said that many garden centres are now stocking a wider selection as more and more gardeners are learning about and demanding good garden plants.

Many high-street chain stores now stock popular shrubs and these are often very reasonably priced, since they are quite small specimens. It is best to buy from a chain store as soon as the plants have been delivered, as they will then be fresh. They have quite a short shelf-life in the warm dry atmosphere of a supermarket.

The great advantage of garden centres is that you can buy and plant shrubs at any time of year as they are sold in containers – pots or flexible polythene bags. Many people like to buy shrubs when they are in flower, so that they know exactly what they are buying. There is a trend today in the garden-centre trade of selling large plants in containers. These, of course, are a lot more expensive than plants in normal-sized pots, but they give instant effect.

You should choose large specimens with care though, for some can be false economy. For instance, it is a sheer waste of money to buy large specimens of quick-growing shrubs like philadelphus or buddleia. However, it is well worth considering larger specimens of slow growers like dwarf conifers, rhododendrons, camellias and so on. Tiny plants of these would take many years to create an impact in your garden. With large specimens of these you are paying for time. Also bear in mind that it is rather a waste of money buying two-year-old heathers, at about twice the price of one-year-olds, for they are quick growers.

CHAPTER 4

PLANTING SHRUBS

The secret of success with shrubs is to plant them properly and that means in deeply dug soil whose texture has been suitably improved. Few shrubs will grow in waterlogged or poorly drained soil and if you have that type you will have to work harder to obtain success with shrubs (or any other plants for that matter), than you would with well-drained soil.

Generally speaking, drainage can be considerably improved by double digging (deep digging) as described below. However, in gardens which become severely waterlogged it is advisable to install a drainage system. Today this is easily achieved, without much disruption of the garden, by laying modern narrow land-drainage tubes. Basically these consist of a long plastic core surrounded by a geotextile filter fabric. They are light, flexible and easy to lay in narrow slit trenches, needing no aggregate backfill as traditional clay land drain pipes do. They can be laid in a herringbone pattern over the site with the main drain leading to a soakaway at the lowest point – a deep hole filled with rubble, at least 1.8 m (6 ft) deep and 1 m (3 ft) wide. The suppliers provide full instructions.

PREPARING THE SHRUB BORDER

If you are devoting a largish area, say a border, to shrubs, it is far better to prepare the entire site than an individual planting position for each shrub. The plants will do better and the spaces between them will be in a suitable condition for planting other subjects, too, like ground cover plants, perennials and bulbs.

To prepare the ground you need to dig it deeply and thoroughly, and though this may seem hard work at the time, once it has been done and the border planted you will not have to do it again. And you can be certain that, all other things being right, the shrubs will get away to a good start. If you don't prepare the ground properly they may take years to become established. The normal sequence of events is that the shrubs put on a little top growth and a lot of root growth during their first year; in the second year they grow vigorously and in the third year they settle down to flowering, and will go on flowering with increasing freedom each succeeding year.

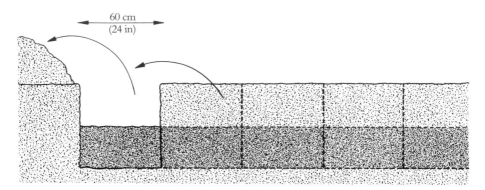

60 cm
(24 in)

Fig 2 Double digging, essential if one is preparing a shrub border, and much to be preferred to digging individual holes for each of the shrubs in the border. The operation is described in detail in the text.

The area to be occupied by the border should be marked out with pegs and in general it is better to have a curving edge than a straight line. Provided the curves are not too sharp this will not make it any more difficult to mow the lawn and the general effect will be far more pleasing.

The soil should be double dug – that is, to twice the depth of the spade blade (Fig. 2). Start at one end of the border by removing a 60 cm (24 in) wide trench to the depth of the spade blade and barrow the soil to the other end of the border, near where the final trench will be. Then get into the trench and dig the soil in the bottom to the depth of the spade blade – or use a fork if the soil is very hard and compacted. It is this compaction which often causes waterlogging. There is no need to turn the soil over – simply break it up.

The next stage is to take out a second trench (of the same width), immediately behind the first, at the same time throwing the soil forward into the first and turning over each spadeful. Then again get into the trench and break up the soil. Proceed in this way until the border has been dug and fill the final trench with the soil removed from the first.

To give the shrubs the best possible start in life, and to improve the texture and drainage of the soil, you would be well advised to mix some well-rotted farmyard manure, or garden compost, into the soil in the bottom of each trench. As a guide, about a quarter of a small barrowload will be sufficient for each 1.2 m (4 ft) length of trench. If you cannot get manure or compost, use peat or pulverized bark, both of which are a bit more expensive. Cheaper would be spent hops or spent mushroom compost (but do not use the latter if you have acid soil, for it contains lumps of chalk).

Lime-hating shrubs like the rhododendrons, camellias and heathers should not be given manure or garden compost. The soil for these is better prepared with peat or leafmould. As well as adding it to the bottom of the trenches during digging, also mix peat or leafmould with the topsoil; and give the plants a thick mulch with one of these materials after planting.

The best time to dig is autumn. The soil can then lie rough over winter when the frost, snow and rains will improve its texture greatly. You can then plant in the spring. It is never a good plan to plant straight into a newly dug border the moment you have finished digging it but rather give the soil time to settle. If you want to plant in the autumn, which is probably the best time to plant shrubs, you need to prepare the soil in the spring, and hoe it during the summer to keep weeds under control.

PLANTING SPECIMENS

If you want to plant a specimen shrub in a lawn or in a gap in the patio, you still need to prepare the ground properly. For an average type of shrub you need to excavate a circle not less than 1.2 m (4 ft) in diameter and dig it to a depth of at least 45 cm (18 in). The procedure is firstly to remove the turf and put this to one side, then remove the topsoil and put that in a separate heap. The sides of the hole should be almost vertical and

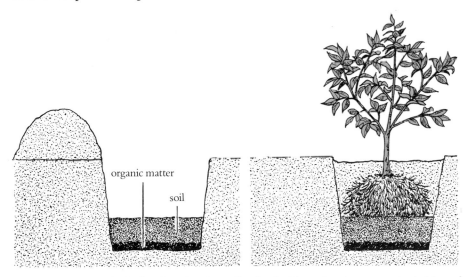

organic matter

soil

Fig 3 Preparing a hole for the planting of a shrub. Note the almost vertical sides of the hole, the flat bottom and the layer of old manure or good compost added to the bottom of the hole to give the plant a good start in its new home.

the bottom flat. The soil at the bottom of the hole should be broken up and manure added, and you then place the turves upside down in the bottom of the hole. Finally the topsoil can be replaced, improving it if necessary with peat of leaf-mould.

WEEDS

It is particularly important if you are planning a shrub border to make sure you eradicate perennial weeds – bindweed, couchgrass, ground elder, etc. If you do not get rid of them completely before you plant you may never get rid of them because it will be almost impossible to deal with them effectively once they become established among shrubs.

The best approach is to spray the weeds with suitable weedkiller in the spring and summer, while they are in full growth, before you start digging. For broad-leaved weeds like bindweed and ground elder use a weedkiller containing glyphosate. For couchgrass and other perennial weed grasses choose a weedkiller containing alloxydim sodium. Use these strictly according to the makers' instructions. Persistent weeds may need a second application, once they have produced new growth.

WHEN TO PLANT

For the purposes of planting, shrubs can be divided into container-grown plants, as bought from a garden centre, and bare-root plants as lifted from a nurseryman's field. Conifers and other evergreens which are field grown are not exactly supplied bare-root but they are root-balled – that is, they have a ball of soil around the roots which is held securely in place with a hessian or plastic-mesh wrap. They come in the same category, though, as bare-root plants for planting purposes.

Container-grown plants can be planted at any time of year provided the ground is not very wet or frozen. It is essential to keep the soil around the roots intact and to water the plants regularly if the weather is dry.

Bare-root deciduous shrubs are supplied and planted when they are completely dormant – between late autumn and late winter. Do not plant them if the ground is very wet or frozen though, but heel them in (plant them temporarily) in a spare piece of ground which is not too wet.

Conifers and other evergreens which are supplied root-balled are best planted in mid- to late spring when the soil is warming up, or in late summer/early autumn while the ground is still warm. They establish very much more quickly if planted when the soil is warm – new roots soon grow into the surrounding soil. If planted in cold wet soil new roots are not produced for a long time and the plants could die.

As a general rule, plants which are on the tender side are best planted in spring so that they have the whole summer to settle down before facing their first winter. Shrubs which have fleshy roots, such as magnolias, are also best planted in late spring or early summer.

PLANTING DISTANCES

It is very easy to overplant a shrub border and it is always a shame when this is done, for then the shrubs grow into each other and it is not possible to enjoy the shape and form of each one. To avoid this one needs to peg out the ground, using a different peg for each shrub. It is always a help if you have worked this out on paper first – preferably squared graph paper with each square representing a foot.

The counsel of perfection is to find out how big each plant will grow and then plant the shrubs so that they will just meet up without growing into each other. This is not as easy to do as it sounds since the same shrub will grow larger or smaller in different parts of the country, depending on soil, climate and other factors.

The simplest rule is to plant large-growing shrubs 1.8 m (6 ft) apart, medium-sized shrubs 1 m (3 ft) apart, and small shrubs 45–60 cm (18 in to 2 ft) apart – but if you use small shrubs plant them in groups of three or five rather than singly: they will be far more effective.

If you follow this advice you will find that the border looks very bare at first. Don't worry, for if you have done your groundwork properly, in a season or two the shrubs will start to fill out and occupy the space allotted to them. Meanwhile you can fill the gaps with bedding plants or bulbs, or work out some ground-cover scheme which can be of permanent value.

PLANTING TECHNIQUES

Unless you buy your shrubs from a garden centre or local nursery they will arrive by post, lorry or rail, neatly packed. If you have to sign a chit, sign it 'unexamined': unless you do that you will have no come-back on anyone if the plants have been badly packaged or unduly long in reaching you.

Once you've got your package unwrap it in the garage or garden shed. The first thing to do is check all the labels to make sure they bear the names of all the plants you ordered. Assuming that they do, you should then examine the shrubs to make sure, to the best of your ability, that they actually are what their labels claim them to be. Very few nurserymen ever send out shrubs wrongly labelled but mistakes do happen. If you think you have been sent the wrong plant, ring the nurseryman at once, and immediately follow up your phone call with a letter.

Magnolias are probably the most exotic-looking of all shrubs. They are not as difficult to grow as many people think. The one shown here is *Magnolia* × *soulangiana*.

The next thing to do is see whether the shrubs have become unduly dry during their journey. If they have stand them in a bucket of water for a couple of hours. Often you will not need to do this.

Next examine the shrubs critically. Sometimes you will find that a few roots have been broken or damaged in lifting at the nursery. Damaged roots do not heal well and can give a shrub a considerable set-back. Any damaged roots should be pruned cleanly away, so that the cut surface will face downwards once the shrub is planted. A clean cut like this will heal quickly, causing the shrub little set-back.

Having examined the roots for obvious damage, the next thing is to examine the whole shrub. What you are looking for is a balance between top growth and root growth. If roots have been left behind in the soil when the shrub was lifted you may have to remove some top growth to balance this. As a general principle it is always worth removing some of the top growth when planting deciduous shrubs and it is usually recommended that they should be cut back by about one third of their size. Conifers and other evergreens do not need this pruning and will usually only have had their coarse holding roots damaged, not their fine feeding roots.

If you do not have time to plant the shrubs straight away, or if the ground is very wet or frozen, they should be heeled in. This is done by taking out a shallow V-shaped trench and putting the plants obliquely into it. Cover the roots with soil. They are then easily lifted when you are ready to plant them.

When it comes to the actual planting there are two rules of tremendous importance. The first is that the hole should be sufficiently large to accommodate the roots without any of them having to be cramped or folded to get them in. The other is that the shrub should be planted to precisely the same depth in the soil as it was in the nursery: if it is planted deeper soil will cover part of the main stem that was never meant to be underground. With field-grown shrubs you will find a soil mark at the base of the stems – use this as a guide to depth when planting. The top of the soil mark should be at ground level.

Having opened up the hole, hold the shrub in it to make sure that all its roots will fit in easily (Fig. 3). From there on you really need two people, one holding the shrub at its correct planting height, the other filling in with soil. The soil should be returned round the roots in layers about 8 or 10 cm (3 or 4 in) thick and each layer should be firmly trodden down with the heel of your boot. The easiest way of making sure that the planting level will be correct is to lay a lath across the hole, since this will show you where your soil will reach once the hole has been filled in.

With container-grown and root-balled shrubs you should take out a hole only slightly wider than the root-ball and of such a depth that after planting the top of the rootball is only slightly below soil level – no more than 12 mm ($\frac{1}{2}$ in). The container or root-wrap must be removed extremely carefully to avoid damaging roots or causing soil to fall away. If roots and soil are disturbed the growth of the plant may be checked. Place the plant in the centre of the hole and then return fine soil in the space between the root-ball and the sides of the hole, firming with your heel as you proceed.

A word about planting mixtures. In recent years several brands have become available which consist of peat with fertilizers added. Their purpose is to encourage the rapid establishment of newly planted shrubs. The use of a planting mixture is therefore highly recommended, particularly if you have a very poor soil. Fork some into the bottom of the planting hole and mix some more with the soil which is to be returned around the plant.

If you want to make your own planting mixture, simply mix a handful of sterilized bonemeal into a large bucketful of peat. But not for lime-hating plants – use hoof and horn meal instead.

AFTERCARE

If the soil starts to become dry after planting, the shrubs should be well watered. This should be repeated as necessary for at least the first year, until the plants are well established. With shallow-rooting shrubs, such as rhododendrons, you should never allow the soil to dry out at any time.

Newly planted evergreens should ideally be sprayed with plain water daily for the first six weeks after planting, as this helps establishment. Conifers particularly appreciate this treatment. It will not be necessary, of course, if the weather is wet. Alternatively, use one of the proprietary anti-transpirant sprays, which come in aerosol form. Follow the manufacturer's instructions closely.

Some tall shrubs, such as brooms and camellias, and certain conifers like cupressus and x cupressocyparis, will benefit from being supported with a stout bamboo cane or stake after planting, until they become established. This prevents the wind from whipping them around so they become loose in the soil.

The soil around shrubs should be kept free from weeds, for dense weed growth can seriously retard their growth. The best way of achieving this is by mulching. This involves covering the ground with a 5–8 cm (2–3 in) layer of peat, leafmould or pulverized (shredded) bark. Do not allow the mulch to reach right up to the stems of the shrubs. Birds are inclined to scavenge through a mulch and you should check periodically

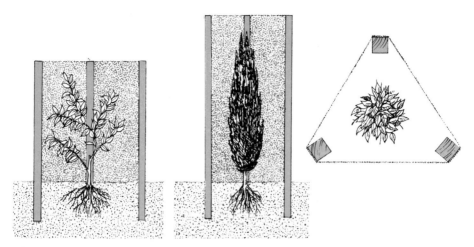

Fig 4 Protecting a newly planted evergreen from winter winds. It is the cold winds from the north and east that usually kill young evergreens, rather than sheer degrees of frost. Insert three stout stakes in the ground and nail hessian or sacking to them.

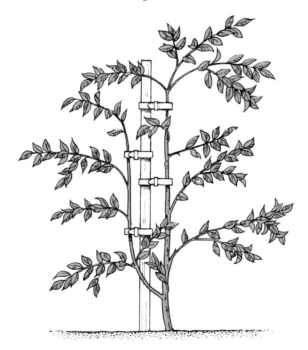

Fig 5 Staking a young shrub. This is particularly important for evergreens, the example shown here being a camellia. Unless staked wind can cause the young shrubs to rock, which can in turn prevent the roots from becoming established.

There are many varieties of *Hibiscus syriacus* with flowers in shades of pink, blue and white. These shrubs are at their best in late summer and early autumn.

to see whether or not they have thrown the mulch up around the stems of the shrubs – or even over them if they are dwarf kinds like heathers. It is well worth topping up a mulch annually in the spring. Mulching not only suppresses weeds but helps to conserve soil moisture. It's particularly appreciated by surface-rooting shrubs like rhododendrons.

If you do not use a mulch then at least consider using a suitable weed-killer to prevent the germination of weed seeds. Such weedkillers are based on simazine or propachlor, the former being the longest-lasting. Such weedkillers must be applied to completely weed-free, moist soil and thereafter the soil surface must not be disturbed. As always, follow the manufacturer's instructions on use to the letter, to avoid any possible damage to plants.

Newly planted conifers and other evergreens should if necessary be protected from cold drying winds during the winter (at least during their first winter). The cold winds from the north and east can kill young ever-greens. As the plants establish and become larger, they also toughen up and are then better able to cope with adverse weather conditions. It is an easy matter to provide protection around newly planted specimens. Insert three stout stakes in the ground, partially around the plant on the windward side, and then nail windbreak netting to them. This screen should be well above the height of the shrub or conifer (Fig. 4).

CHAPTER 5

PRUNING

There are two ways of pruning shrubs: the right way and the wrong way. Of the two the second is by far the more commonly practised. It consists basically of going out with a pair of secateurs and giving shrubs 'a good haircut' because some inner urge tells you that it might be a good idea to do so. Such pruning may satisfy an inner urge, but it will do the shrubs no good.

The right way to prune a shrub is to note whether it flowers on wood of the current season's growth, or on wood of the previous season's growth. This is easily established by examining the plant when in flower. If it flowers on wood of the current season's growth (and this includes most of the shrubs which flower after mid-summer), the shoots that have flowered are cut hard back in early spring before growth starts to encourage plenty of new growth. If it flowers on wood of the previous season's growth (which includes most of the shrubs which flower in spring and early summer), the whole shoot which has flowered should be cut back immediately after flowering.

When pruning it is always worth remembering *why* one is pruning. The purpose of pruning is to promote the production of healthy flowering or fruiting wood. It may also serve the additional purpose of keeping the shrub tidy.

It would be completely wrong to think that all shrubs need pruning and must fit into one or other of the two categories described above. The simple fact is that the great majority of shrubs never need pruning. Pruning techniques are given, as applicable, in the descriptive lists.

There is one operation which is sometimes described as pruning (though it scarcely amounts to that) and that is dead-heading. This simply involves removing dead flower heads. In the case of rhododendrons this is done by picking the trusses off between thumb and finger, but with lilacs and many other shrubs this needs to be done with secateurs. The purpose of dead-heading is to prevent the shrub from putting all its energy into producing unwanted seeds, which would diminish its crop of flowers the following year. It is always worth dead-heading any shrub for which this treatment is recommended.

As for tools for pruning, all one needs is a good pair of secateurs. There

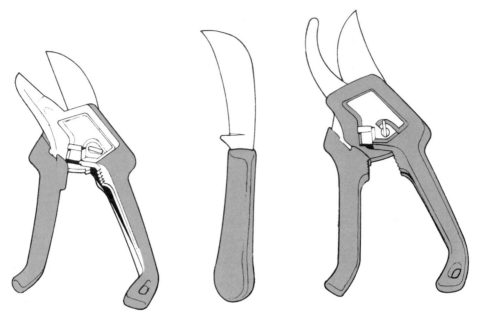

Fig 6 Pruning tools. Though there are dozens of different pruning tools on the market, the ones shown here are all one normally needs. Left, anvil type secateurs, centre, a pruning knife and, right, the classic parrot's beak type of secateurs.

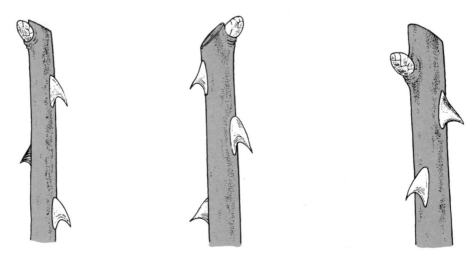

Fig 7 Pruning cuts. Left, the cut correctly made: centre, the cut made too close to the bud which could damage it and, right, the cut made too high above the bud, which will result in that wood dying back to the bud.

are two basic types of secateurs on the market – though there are several variations on both kinds – the parrot-bill and the anvil type. With the parrot-bill type the blades cut by crossing each other: with the anvil type the cut is made by one blade closing against a flat surface. It really does not matter in the least which you have: what does matter is that they are sharp. Use a small oilstone to keep the blades sharp. Blunt secateurs do endless damage. Like all good tools, secateurs should be treated with respect: never try to cut anything that is too big for them to cut easily, and never twist the secateurs while cutting. If you have any thick wood to cut then use a pair of long-handled, heavy-duty pruners, which can cut through stems at least 2.5 cm (1 in) thick. Or use a pruning saw.

CHAPTER 6

INCREASING SHRUBS

It is the creativeness of increasing plants that makes it such fun – at once so much of a challenge and ·so rewarding when one is successful. Certainly most keen gardeners increase their plants just for the fun of it, but it has a useful function too. If you have a shrub that you think is really outstanding and you want more of it, try propagating it yourself rather than buying new plants: you will be far more satisfied with the results. You may also find that other people are often asking for a piece of one of your shrubs: try propagating it yourself, then you'll have the pleasure of being able to give young plants away: you may even find other people who enjoy increasing their plants, and then you will be able to swap one good thing for another.

The majority of shrubs are easy to increase. Unfortunately, the more difficult they are to propagate the more expensive they are to buy, and in many ways one would gain most by being able to increase the difficult ones. That will come with practice.

There are four main ways in which shrubs are increased: seeds, cuttings, layering and grafting. Of these grafting is used only for a small number of shrubs and is too specialised a subject to cover here. If you want a comprehensive guide to the techniques of plant raising you should obtain *The Complete Book of Plant Propagation* by Robert C. M. Wright and Alan Titchmarsh (published by Ward Lock Ltd).

SEEDS

This is the easiest and cheapest way of raising shrubs and it is surprising how many can be increased in this way: it is also surprising how young some of them will flower – many in their third year from seed. Indeed, anyone planning a shrub garden on a shoestring would do well to consider the idea of growing as much as possible from seed.

Yet one must be aware of the problems. Species or wild plants will come true from seed, but hybrids will not. If you don't know that you may well be very disappointed by the results. For example, if you sow seed of a named variety of almost any shrub you should expect the seedlings to be inferior to it. If you sow seed of a variegated shrub do not expect the seedlings to be variegated: it is highly unlikely that they will be. And if you sow seed of a hybrid the resulting seedlings will almost certainly be inferior to the plant from which you obtained the seed, a proportion reverting to one parent, and a proportion reverting to the other parent. The chances of your getting something even better are, frankly, negligible.

Of course, you can collect your own seeds if you have any species in your garden. Seeds in dry pods and capsules should be gathered just before the 'containers' split open and shed the seeds. Lay them out on a sheet of newspaper in a warm sunny dry place for a couple of weeks. Then remove the seeds from the capsules and store them in envelopes until the spring.

Berries – like those of cotoneasters, berberis and roses – are treated in a different way. Collect when ripe and lightly crush them to expose the seeds. Then place layers of them between layers of moist sand in an old tin with drainage holes in the bottom, or in pots. Stand these under a north-facing wall or fence for the winter, where they will be subjected to hard frosts. Then sow in the spring – but do not try to separate the seeds from the sand. Sow the whole lot.

Bear in mind that seeds of some shrubs (particularly those of berrying shrubs) can take at least a year to germinate after sowing so you will have to be patient. On the other hand seeds of many other shrubs germinate in a matter of weeks or in a few months. So if nothing appears after a year or so, do not discard the seeds but give them more time – at least another year. You can buy a good range of shrub seeds from many of our leading seedsmen – at a fraction of the cost of buying plants from a garden centre. So send off for their catalogues and see what's on offer.

With many hardy shrubs the seeds can be sown in the open ground where they will germinate satisfactorily. But for the amateur this is not really the best way of going about raising shrubs from seed. The best practice is to sow the seeds in pots, which can be clearly labelled, and which can moreover be gathered together in one part of the garden, possibly in a frame if you have one, where they can more easily be protected from birds, mice, rabbits and other creatures that have the irritating habit of digging them up or eating them.

Pots should be properly crocked with bits of broken pot placed over the hole at the bottom – clay pots are generally preferable to plastic pots because they are porous – and some coarse peat placed over them.

Use John Innes seed compost for sowing, though not for lime-hating plants which need an acid compost. Seeds of plants like rhododendrons can be sown in pure peat. Seeds should be covered with a layer of compost which roughly equals twice their diameter. Very fine seeds, though, like those of rhododendrons, should not be covered but simply pressed into the compost surface with a flat piece of wood.

The pots are best plunged to their rims in sand or weathered ashes in a well-ventilated cold frame. Make sure the compost does not dry out at any time.

Once the seeds have germinated prick them out individually into small pots – say 9 cm (3½ in) pots, using John Innes potting compost No. 1, or an acid soilless compost for lime haters. The seedlings can be grown on in the frame until they are large enough to plant out, meantime potting them on into larger pots as necessary.

CUTTINGS

Cuttings are the most commonly used of all methods of increasing shrubs. There are three different types of cuttings used and, although many books tell you that you use one type for one shrub and another type for another shrub, in practice it does not always work out quite as simply as that. For one thing, it takes judgement to tell at precisely which moment the cutting is ready to be taken. The general rule, if in doubt which type of cutting to take, is to try soft cuttings first, then half-ripe cuttings and finally hardwood cuttings – as the three different types are called – in that order.

SOFT CUTTINGS

These are cuttings taken from the growing tips of the shoots and trimmed just below a node (a node is the point at which leaves occur on the shoot). The best time to take cuttings of this type (Fig. 8) is during late spring and early summer when growth is most active, which will give well-established plants by autumn.

The easiest way of taking the cuttings is to remove them from the parent plant with a 'heel' (a piece of the old wood) by pulling downwards and outwards. The cutting can then be trimmed with a new razor blade below the node to a length of about 8 cm (3 in) and dipped in hormone rooting powder. If used discreetly it helps rooting, but if used in excess it tends to retard it. The cuttings should then be inserted round the edge of a pot, each cutting being slipped into a small hole made with a dibber and then well firmed. It is important to ensure that the bottom of the cutting and all the parts below the surface are in contact with the soil, and this is done by pushing the dibber down into the soil beside the cutting. A suitable compost for rooting cuttings consists of a mixture of equal parts sphagnum peat and coarse sand, or a mixture of equal parts peat and Perlite.

The great problem with soft cuttings is simply that they are soft: the wood has not hardened, and indeed the leaves are still delicate and the cutting is therefore liable to wilt. To prevent this it needs to be kept in close, humid conditions, ideally in an electrically heated propagating case in the greenhouse. Alternatively enclose each pot in a clear polythene bag (supporting the bag with short split canes) and stand it on a windowsill in a warm room indoors, but out of direct sun (Fig. 9).

Check the cuttings regularly. If any are showing signs of rotting, remove them immediately and spray the rest with a fungicide such as benomyl.

Fig 8 (*a*) Soft tip cuttings being taken below a node. (*b*) the cutting showing what needs to be done to prepare it for planting and (*c*) the prepared cutting ready for inserting in the rooting medium, where it should root if kept warm and humid for 10–14 days.

Fig 9 Pot of cuttings enclosed in a polythene bag.

HALF-RIPE CUTTINGS

Cuttings of this type are generally easier to root than softwood cuttings since they are less liable to wilt. However, although the base of the cutting – the part which will root – will have become woody, the growing end will still be soft enough to wilt, so some care is still needed in handling them.

Half-ripe cuttings are taken between early summer and early autumn and can be taken with a heel. This is most easily achieved by pushing your thumb firmly into the angle between the new growth (the cutting) and the old wood. The cutting will come away with quite a large piece of the old wood and bark attached to it (Fig. 10). The heel needs to be trimmed with a razor blade to get rid of the loose bark and to give it a clean, flat face. It should not simply be planted straight from the shrub without this tidying up.

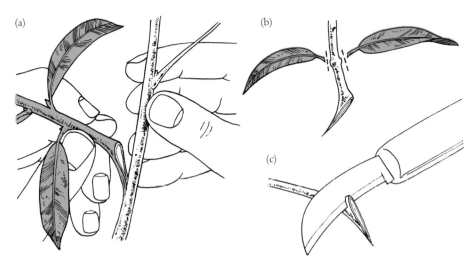

Fig 10 (*a*) Half-ripe cuttings being taken with a heel: this is done by pulling the cuttings downwards and outwards from the old wood of the shrub. (*b*) the cutting with the lower leaves removed. (*c*) the base of the cutting being trimmed ready for planting.

Alternatively you can prepare nodal cuttings, as described for soft-woods. Whether you take heel or nodal cuttings, remove the leaves from the lower third of the cutting, then dip the base in hormone rooting powder. If a heel cutting is excessively long, the top can be trimmed. Cuttings of most plants should be between 10 and 15 cm (4 and 6 in) long. Heathers can be propagated from heel cuttings, which will be about 5 cm (2 in) long.

When prepared, the cuttings are inserted in pots in exactly the same way as softwoods. However they do not need such warm, close conditions and can be rooted in a cold frame, or on the bench in a cool greenhouse. Cuttings of some kinds (heathers, for instance) will root in a matter of weeks while others will take many months. Some may not be well rooted until spring of the following year. But when rooted pot off into small pots and grow on as for softwoods.

HARDWOOD CUTTINGS

These are the easiest of all cuttings to prepare and root. They are taken when the leaves have fallen, using current year's shoots which are thoroughly ripe and woody. Cut these shoots into 15–30 cm (6–12 in) lengths. The soft tip of the shoot is discarded. The top cut of the cutting should be made immediately above a dormant bud and the bottom cut just below a bud. Use secateurs for preparing hardwoods. Dip bases of cuttings in hormone rooting powder.

Hardwood cuttings are generally rooted in a well-drained sheltered spot out of doors, but can also be rooted in the soil in a well-ventilated cold frame. Take out a V-shaped trench and stand the cuttings along this about 15 cm (6 in) apart (Fig. 11). You can put some coarse sand in the bottom of the trench. The cuttings should be inserted to two-thirds of their length. Return fine soil around them and firm it really well with your heel. They may need to be refirmed after hard frosts which tend to loosen them in the soil. The cuttings should be well rooted by the following autumn, when they can be lifted and planted elsewhere in the garden.

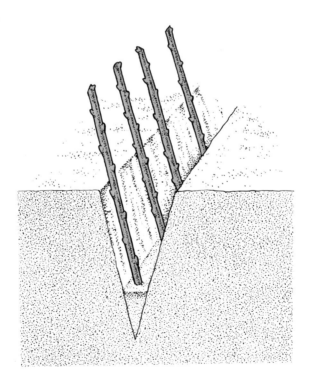

Fig 11 Hardwood cuttings lined out in a V-shaped trench with some sharp sand in the bottom.

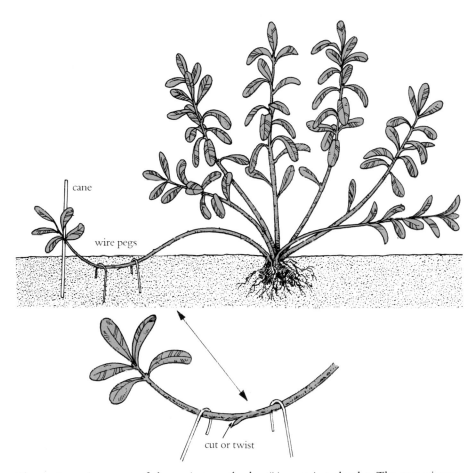

cane

wire pegs

cut or twist

Fig 12 Layering, one of the easiest methods of increasing shrubs. The top picture shows a suitable branch pegged into the ground. The small drawing below shows how the branch is wounded to encourage rooting.

LAYERING

Almost any shrub whose branches can be brought down to the ground can be increased by layering. The operation is very simple. Firstly you bend the branch down so that it is parallel with the ground: you then put a peg or two into the ground to hold it in that position. Next you take out a 15 cm (6 in) deep hole in the ground, adding some sand to the soil in the bottom. You then bend the shoot down into the hole and peg it

The dwarf Japanese cut-leaf maple *Acer palmatum* 'Dissectum' is one of the showiest of all shrubs grown for their autumn colour.

into position. Next, refill the hole with soil and tie the growing tip of the shoot securely to a cane or stick (Fig. 12). Finally, water the ground in which the shoot has been buried, and place a flat stone over it to prevent moisture from evaporating too fast. Leave well alone until rooted — which will usually take two years for the new plant to be well enough established to move.

The best time of year to carry out layering is mid-summer, but it can be done at almost any time. The best wood to use is year old wood, and the point at which new growth emerges from this is one of the likeliest places for rooting to occur.

Some plants need a little assistance in rooting when layered, and almost anything that will constrict the flow of sap through the layer will help. This can be done by making a slit in the wood to about half its thickness, or by sharply twisting the shoot to break some of the tissue, at the point where the shoot is pegged into the soil. Roots will form where the shoot has been 'wounded'.

CHAPTER 7

DECIDUOUS SHRUBS

Deciduous shrubs lose their leaves in winter. All come from parts of the world that have sharply differentiated seasons, which means in effect cold winters and less-cold summers. They come from climates that are as cold in winter as our own, or often even colder, and the majority can be relied on as being completely hardy. There are some exceptions, including fuchsias and hydrangeas, both of which are safest given a little protection in the winter.

Acer MAPLE

These are grown not for their flowers, which are seldom noticed, but for their foliage and their usually brilliant autumn colouring. They all grow best in sheltered positions in good, moist well-drained soil, with preferably a little shade. *A. japonicum* 'Aureum', 1.2 by 1.2 m (4 by 4 ft) is slow growing with beautiful soft yellow lobed leaves which are exceptional among yellow-leaved deciduous shrubs in that they hold their colour throughout the summer. *A. japonicum* 'Aconitifolium' (*A. j.* 'Laciniatum'), 1.8 by 1.5m (6 by 5 ft), leaves deeply lobed and toothed, green, turning brilliant scarlet in autumn, slow growing but eventually a large shrub. *A. palmatum*, 3.6 by 4.5 m (12 by 15 ft), the Japanese maple, slow growing but ultimately forming a small tree, leaves lobed, colouring brilliantly in autumn. *A. p.* 'Atropurpureum', slower growing, 1.8 by 1.2 m (6 by 4 ft), leaves purple, appearing bright crimson when seen against the light, superb autumn colour. *A. p.* 'Bloodgood' has rich purple-red foliage, 1.8 by 1.5 m (6 by 5 ft). *A. p.* 'Senkaki', the coral-bark maple, has coral-red branches and yellow autumn leaf colour, 3 by 3 m (10 by 10 ft). *A. p.* 'Dissectum', 1 by 1.2 m (3 by 4 ft), forms a low mushroom-shaped shrub, leaves very finely divided, fresh green turning bright orange in autumn, dislikes cold winds. 'Dissectum Atropurpureum' has purple leaves. The two look exceptionally good when planted together. 'Dissectum Garnet' is a new variety with crimson-purple foliage, 1.2 by 1.2 m (4 by 4 ft). *A. p.* 'Heptalobum Osakazuki', 3 by 3 m (10 by 10 ft), has large lobed green leaves providing some of the most brilliant autumn colour of any shrub, passing through every shade of yellow, orange, scarlet and crimson. *A. negundo* 'Flamingo' is a tree, but can be grown as a shrub if pruned annually in early spring. The leaves are variegated pink, white and green, 3 by 3 m (10 by 10 ft).

Aralia ANGELICA TREE

Not really trees at all, but growing to 3 m (10 ft) and usually suckering mildly, these shrubs are grown for their huge compound leaves which can be over 1 m (3 ft) long and for their enormous plumes of white flowers borne in early autumn. Wood is soft and easily cut by frosts, but this seldom kills the plants. The green leaved *A. elata* is not particularly good; infinitely better are *A. e.* 'Aureovariegata' (yellow variegated) and *A. e.* 'Variegata' (white variegated). Sandy soil.

Artemisia

Known variously as lad's love, southernwood or old man, the most shrubby of the family is *A. abrotanum* which is grown primarily for the silvery-grey, finely divided feathery foliage – like lace. Usually rather untidy, becomes a neat, rounded dome if cut hard down each spring; 1 by 1.2 m (3 by 4 ft). *A. arborescens* is similar and has even finer silver foliage; 1.2 by 1.2 m (4 by 4 ft). Half-ripe cuttings.

Berberis BARBERRY

A large charming group of both deciduous and evergreen shrubs, all of which are very easy to grow in any soil. All are very spiny. What you finish up with may well depend upon what your local garden centre happens to offer, but the following are among the best deciduous species. *B. × rubrostilla*, 1.8 by 1.8 m (6 by 6 ft), one of the very best, flowers yellow in short panicles in early summer, leaves small, pale green; in autumn the arching branches are covered with masses of red fruits. *B. thunbergii*, 1.5 by 1.8 m (5 by 6 ft) has straw-coloured flowers in early summer and bright red berries and leaves in autumn. *B. t.* 'Atropurpurea' has rich purplish red foliage which turns bright red in autumn: a highly effective foliage plant. There are lots of quite new *thunbergii* varieties, too, like 'Aurea', golden-yellow foliage; 'Dart's Purple', purple-red leaves; 'Dart's Red Lady', very deep purple; 'Kobold', bright green with good autumn colour; and 'Rose Glow' with purple foliage and rose-pink young growth. All of these are small shrubs, not above 1 m (3 ft) in height. *B. wilsoniae,* 1 by 1.2 m (3 by 4 ft), is very spiny; the flowers are rather dull yellow, early summer, followed by great ropes of glowing coral berries in autumn. The leaves are soft, small and turn red and orange in autumn. *B. × ottawensis* 'Purpurea' is a tall vigorous shrub to at least 3 m (10 ft) with a spread of 2.4 m (8 ft); it has large rich purple foliage. Increase berberis by seed (but seedlings may be variable) or, better, from half-ripe cuttings.

Buddleia BUTTERFLY BUSH

Fast-growing shrubs valued for their late flowering, growing well in any soil but preferring a sunny site. The ever-popular butterfly bush is *B. davidii*, 4.5 m (15 ft), producing dense spikes of flowers in late summer. The darkest is 'Black Knight', with deep violet flowers; 'Empire Blue' is rich violet-blue; 'Harlequin' has cream-variegated leaves and red-purple flowers; 'Peace' is white; 'Pink Pearl' lilac-pink; and 'Royal Red' is a favourite red-purple variety. Prune hard early each spring, cutting right back to the last pair of buds on each of the previous season's shoots. *B. alternifolia*, 4.5 by 4.5 m (15 by 15 ft), is very different in appearance, producing lilac-mauve flowers in clusters all along the arching twigs through early summer. It has small willow-shaped leaves and a stronger scent than any other buddleia. Flowers quite well when left unpruned but is even better when shoots that have flowered are removed immediately after flowering. Hardwood cuttings.

Callicarpa

Uncommon shrubs grown for their unusual berries and equally unusual autumn foliage. *C. bodinieri giraldii*, 1.8 by 1.8 m (6 by 6 ft), leaves and stems downy, pale pink flowers late summer, autumn colour pink and mauve, the bare branches covered in bright violet berries. The variety 'Profusion' bears an even heavier crop of berries. Seed; half-ripe cuttings.

Caryopteris BLUE SPIRAEA

Only one species, *C. clandonensis*, is grown, 1.2 by 1.2 m (4 by 4 ft). A grey-leaved shrub prized for its pure blue flowers borne in terminal spikes from late summer until early autumn. The variety 'Heavenly Blue' has deeper blue flowers and is a somewhat smaller, more compact shrub. Best grown in groups and makes an ideal partner for fuchsias. Needs full sun and well drained soil; may get killed in a hard winter, especially if the ground gets very wet. Prune hard in early spring to the last pair of buds on the previous season's growth. Soft or half-ripe cuttings.

Ceanothus CALIFORNIAN LILAC

The deciduous ceanothus are far hardier than the evergreen ones, but never achieve that richness of blue for which this genus is famed, the flowers being a rather muddy colour. The two best are 'Gloire de Versailles' with sky blue flowers, and 'Topaz' with slightly deeper blue flowers. 1.8 by 1.8 m (6 by 6 ft). Prune hard back to within two buds of the last season's growth each spring. Flowers are produced in large trusses from early summer till autumn, with two main flushes. Half-ripe cuttings late summer.

Universally known simply as 'Japonica', the flowering quince *Chaenomeles speciosa* is a highly effective flowering shrub. It is available in a wide range of colours.

Ceratostigma

One species, *C. willmottianum*, is grown for its very pure blue flowers produced from late summer until the frosts. It mixes well with fuchsias and the shrubby potentillas. 90 cm (3ft), usually less. It is only semi-woody and the winter's frosts will usually kill it back to or near ground level. *C. plumbaginoides* is a much smaller shrub, suitable for a rock garden, producing a succession of blue flowers from mid-summer to late autumn. Division or half-ripe cuttings.

Chaenomeles JAPANESE QUINCE

Known to countless generations of gardeners simply as 'Japonica', it is one of those annoying plants whose names are constantly being changed by botanists. It has been known as cydonia and more recently as *Chaenomeles lagenaria* but is now *Chaenomeles speciosa*. Under whatever name it is a good garden shrub with a dense, tangled habit of growth. Shy flowering when young, it soon settles down to producing a good show every year. It flowers most freely in full sun. In a sheltered position it will start flowering in mid-winter, building up to its best in mid-spring. Vigorous forms grow up to 3 m (10 ft). There are several good varieties like 'Cardinalis', crimson-scarlet; 'Geisha Girl', salmon-pink; 'Moerloosei', pink and white; 'Nivalis', pure white; and 'Rosea Plena', rose-pink, double. Propagate by layering.

Chimonanthus WINTERSWEET

C. praecox is one of the most delightful winter-flowering shrubs, producing its pale yellow, scarlet-throated flowers from late autumn until early spring. The scent is even more marvellous. Leaves large, bright green turning yellow in autumn. Young plants take time to settle down to flowering. 3 by 1.8 m (10 by 6 ft). Seed or layers.

Chionanthus FRINGE TREE

Seldom tree-like, *C. virginicus* is grown for its drooping fringe-like panicles of scented white flowers which are borne early to mid-summer, but only on established plants. Leaves long, pointed, turning yellow in autumn. 3 by 2.4 m (10 by 8 ft). Seed or layering.

Cornus DOGWOOD

A large family and a very mixed bunch. Some are grown for their winter bark, some for their variegated leaves and some for their flowers.

For bark There are two outstanding species. *C. alba* 'Sibirica' produces the brightest red young shoots of any shrub. Also with red stems are *C. alba* 'Elegantissima' with white-variegated foliage, and *C. alba* 'Spaethii' with gold-variegated leaves. For contrast plant *C. stolonifera* 'Flaviramea' which has brilliant yellow young stems. To get the best colouring on the young stems cut the plants hard back to old wood in early spring. Both plants will grow in very boggy conditions, literally with their feet in water.

For variegation C. *alternifolia* 'Variegata' is one of the finest of all variegated shrubs, with small leaves richly marked with white. It has a neat twiggy habit and needs no pruning. 3 by 1.8 m (10 by 6 ft).

For flower The Cornelian cherry, C. *mas*, is useful for its abundance of small yellow flowers in early spring. These are followed by red oval fruits which make an excellent conserve. There are three variegated forms, all good: 'Aurea', variegated gold; 'Elegantissima' variegated yellow and pink; and 'Variegata', leaves margined white. Good autumn colour on poor soil.

The other flowering dogwoods are very different. The flower is surrounded by large showy bracts (modified leaves which are coloured and look like petals). Of these the most reliable is C. *kousa*, with pointed white bracts which slowly turn pink, produced during early summer and lasting a good six weeks. C. *kousa chinensis* has even larger bracts. Curious red raspberry-like fruits are produced in late summer and autumn colour is good on fertile soils. Mature plants develop a tiered habit, with flat, tabular branches upon which the flowers appear to dance, held upright on long stalks. Slow growing to 4.5 by 3 m (15 by 10 ft). C. *nuttallii* is even finer, with larger bracts and delicate autumn colouring, but it needs an acid soil and a sheltered position. C. *florida* is similar to C. *kousa* but less reliable and easily hit by late frosts; the bracts are twisted in a curious manner. C. *florida* 'Rubra' has pink bracts and is even better. The wood needs a good ripening if the shrub is to flower well. 4.5 by 4.5 m (15 by 15 ft). No pruning for any of the flowering dogwoods. Increase by hardwood cuttings or layering.

Corylopsis

Another of those treasures with yellow, scented flowers produced early to mid-spring. C. *pauciflora* is generally the best species to grow, producing short hanging spikes of pale primrose open bell-shaped flowers. Height over 1.8 m (6 ft) with similar spread. Also worth growing is C. *willmottiae* 'Spring Purple', of similar stature, but with purple young shoots and fragrant greenish yellow flowers. Corylopsis prefer an acid soil and the shelter afforded by other shrubs. Leaves often colour well in the autumn. Propagate by layering.

Corylus HAZEL AND FILBERT

C. *avellana* 'Contorta', known as Harry Lauder's Walking Stick, is a curious form of the native wild hazel with curled and twisted branches, useful for floral decoration. 3 by 3 m (10 by 10 ft). C. *maxima* 'Purpurea', the purple filbert, has large leaves of a deep, rich purple colour and purple catkins in spring. One of the most dramatic of all purple shrubs; looks best contrasted with a yellow-leaved or variegated shrub, preferably evergreen for contrast. Or why not try it with the yellow-leaved hazel, *C. avellana* 'Aurea', with delightful soft yellow foliage. Prune the coloured-leaved kinds hard each spring to maintain compact shrubs. Propagate by layering or hardwood cuttings.

Cotinus SMOKE BUSH

Formerly included under *Rhus*, these shrubs are quite distinct from that genus, with oval or rounded leaves and great clouds of smoke-like flower heads – hence the common name. Height and spread 3 m (10 ft). Any soil, preferably sun. *C. coggygria* flowers so freely that the whole plant appears to be hidden in a haze of smoke. Brilliant orange and scarlet autumn leaf colour. The variety 'Flame' is even better. Other varieties like 'Foliis Purpureis', 'Notcutt's Variety' and 'Royal Purple' have superb rich purple foliage. Propagate from half-ripe cuttings or, more easily, by layering.

Cotoneaster

A huge family, the best known of which is the herring-bone cotoneaster, *C. horizontalis*, which produces its branches in flat, fish-bone design. If grown against a wall these will press themselves flat against it. It also makes a good ground-cover plant. Leaves tiny, almost round, turning crimson in autumn; masses of bright red berries. The form 'Variegatus' has prettily variegated leaves and is more effective. Layers, seed, half-ripe cuttings.

Cytisus BROOM

Colourful but short-lived shrubs, useful for planting in a new garden to give instant effect. They hate root disturbance and once planted should

Dwarf broom, *Cytisus* × *praecox*, makes a low mound of primrose yellow flowers in spring.

Golden bells or forsythia, one of the most spectacular of spring flowering shrubs. It does particularly well on gravelly soils.

never be moved. Tend to suffer from wind-rock and need to be securely staked all their lives. All have green twigs, minute but deciduous leaves and pea-type flowers. Taller kinds grow to about 1.8 m (6 ft) in height and spread and include 'Burkwoodii' with red and yellow flowers; 'Dorothy Walpole', cerise and crimson; 'Killiney Red', deep velvety red;

'Minstead', white and lilac; *C. scoparius* 'Andreanus', yellow and crimson; *C. s.* 'Cornish Cream', cream; *C. s.* 'Golden Sunlight', rich yellow. There are lots of small brooms, too, like *C.* × *beanii*, golden-yellow; *C.* × *kewensis*, cream; 'Lena', yellow and ruby red; *C.* × *praecox*, rich cream; *C.* × *praecox* 'Allgold', bright yellow; *C. procumbens*, yellow; and 'Zeelandia', cream and pink. The main flowering period of broom is late spring/early summer and all need full sun and very well drained (even dry) soil. Raise from seeds or half-ripe cuttings.

Daphne
Grown primarily for their tremendous fragrance, the daphnes mentioned here are hardy but a bit temperamental, inclined to die on you suddenly without any ascertainable cause. *D. mezereum*, the mezereon, 1.5 by 1.2 m (5 by 4 ft), with erect twigs smothered in early to mid-spring with purplish red or lilac flowers, very strongly scented. 'Alba' has pure white flowers and makes an effective contrast. Its berries are yellow, those of the type plant red. Both form a ready means of increase. Good at the front of the border, and best planted in groups. *Daphne* × *burkwoodii* 'Somerset' is semi-evergreen with sweetly scented pink flowers in late spring/early summer. Height and spread 1.2 m (4 ft). Daphnes thrive in partial or dappled shade. Propagate from half-ripe cuttings, seeds or by layering.

Decaisnea fargesii
Grown primarily for its metallic-blue bean-like seed pods, this is an unusual and striking shrub, with large, pinnate leaves 30 cm (1 ft) long and yellow, pea-type flowers in spring. It forms a tall shrub to 3 m in height, numerous erect stems. Rich moist, well drained soil. Seed.

Deutzia
A very easily grown family of thoroughly reliable early summer-flowering shrubs. All produce erect stems and clusters of small flowers, usually white, occasionally pink. Any soil, sun or slight shade. There are lots of hybrids, like *D.* × *elegantissima*, white, flushed rose, about 1.8 m (6 ft) in height and spread; 'Magicien', white, tinted pink, similar stature; *D.* × *magnifica*, double white flowers in huge trusses, 1.8 m (6 ft) in height and spread; 'Mont Rose', similar stature, rose-pink; *D.* × *rosea*, pink, about 90 cm (3 ft) in height and spread; and *D.* × *rosea* 'Carminea', rose-carmine. Prune out old flowered wood immediately after flowering, right back to where new shoots are being produced. Propagate from half-ripe or hardwood cuttings.

Diervilla
D. × *splendens* is an attractive shrub with its copper-flushed foliage and

sulphur-yellow flowers in summer and early autumn. Height and spread about 90 cm (3 ft). Prune and propagate as for deutzia.

Enkianthus
A shrub for acid soils, *E. campanulatus* has cream and reddish bell-shaped flowers in late spring, and the leaves turn red in autumn. Height in excess of 2.4 m (8 ft), with a spread of at least 1.8 m (6 ft). Ideal for dappled shade with moist peaty soil. Propagate by layering.

Eucryphia
Only one member of this genus is deciduous, *E. glutinosa*. It forms an upright, bushy shrub over 3 by 2.4 m (10 by 8 ft) well clothed to the ground, has pinnate leaves that turn to brilliant oranges and scarlets in autumn, and bears in late summer/early autumn white flowers with delicate buff anthers; the plant when grown well is so smothered in flowers that they hide the foliage. Provide a sheltered sunny position and cool moist acid soil with plenty of peat and leaf-mould added. Half-ripe cuttings (difficult) or layering.

Euonymus SPINDLEBERRY
The charm of the deciduous members of this genus lies in their autumn colouring and in their colourful fruits. *E. europaeus*, a British native, has crimson and scarlet autumn colouring, and pink fruit-cases that split to reveal bright orange seeds. Even better is the variety 'Red Cascade' with really heavy crops of fruit, 3.6 by 2.4 m (12 by 8 ft). Excellent for chalky soils; sun or partial shade. Half-ripe cuttings, layering or seeds.

Exochorda
E. × macrantha 'The Bride' is the best-known of these arching shrubs which are laden in late spring with large single-rose-like flowers. Up to 1.5 m (5 ft) in height and spread. Not suitable for shallow chalky soils. Prune back old flowered shoots after flowering. Soft cuttings or layering.

Forsythia GOLDEN BELLS
Among the brightest of spring-flowering shrubs, renowned for their profusion of golden bell-shaped flowers. All are easy to grow in any fertile soil, preferably in sun. The finest is 'Lynwood', with very rich yellow flowers, 1.8 by 1.8 m (6 by 6 ft); 'Spring Glory', 2.4 by 1.8 m (8 by 6 ft), has larger flowers which smother the branches. *F. suspensa* is a rather rambling pseudo-climber, ideal for using to cover a garden shed, flowers pale yellow. A newish variety of compact habit is 'Golden Nugget' with large bright yellow blooms, 1.5 m (5 ft) in height and spread. Cut back old flowered shoots as soon as flowering is over, to new ones lower down. Half-ripe or hardwood cuttings; layering.

Fuchsia

Among the most charming of late summer flowering shrubs, the fuchsias are hardier than is generally realized. Although they make wood, they behave more like herbaceous plants, the wood usually being killed to ground level in winter. It is best to cut them right down to the ground in early spring. They flower from mid-summer until the frosts. Flower equally well in sun or shade. Among the best are *F. magellanica gracilis*, a little shrub with graceful branches and slender flowers, red and purple. *F. magellanica* is similar but larger flowered. 'Riccartonii' is one of the hardiest with large scarlet and purple flowers. 'Margaret' has very large flowers with reflexed carmine sepals and a frilled petunia skirt. 'Mrs. Popple', also very hardy, with a weeping habit, has large flowers, carmine with a clear violet skirt; 'Tom Thumb' is a compact little dwarf with dainty flowers, carmine and purple. If doubtful as to the hardiness of any you plant, heap some ashes over them through the winter. Increase by soft cuttings.

Fuchsia 'Mrs Popple' is a hardy variety, suitable for growing outdoors in the milder parts of the country, including seaside gardens.

The witch hazels, varieties of *Hamamelis mollis*, are invaluable winter-flowering shrubs and easily grown in acid to neutral soils in partial shade.

Genista BROOM

All have yellow flowers and are generally longer lived than cytisus. Their cultural requirements are the same. The tallest is *G. aetnensis*, the Mount Etna broom, growing to 4.5 by 3 m (15 ft by 10 ft), flowers early to mid-summer and is a blaze of brilliant yellow – looking rather like a golden fountain. *G. lydia* is a complete contrast, reaching only 60 cm (2 ft) but spreading widely in time, flowers bright yellow, early summer. The Spanish gorse, *G. hispanica*, is a very spiny dome-shaped shrub, 1.2 by 2.4 m (4 by 8 ft), with yellow flowers early to mid-summer; hardy only in mild areas. Another dwarf is *G. pilosa* 'Lemon Spreader', with a spreading habit, about 30 cm (12 in) high and golden-yellow flowers in late spring. All need full sun and very well-drained soil. Raise from seeds or half-ripe cuttings.

Hamamelis WITCH HAZEL

The finest of all winter-flowering deciduous shrubs with large hazel-like leaves which colour well in autumn and curiously twisted, strap-shaped petals, usually yellow, red at the base, heavily scented, the flowers lasting for nearly two months. Slow-growing but ultimately tall, often in excess of 3 by 2.4 m (10 by 8 ft). *H. mollis* and its varieties are probably the best known. Good varieties of this are 'Coombe Wood', 'Goldcrest' and sulphur-yellow 'Pallida'. *H.* × *intermedia* varieties can also be recommended: 'Allgold', 'Diane' (coppery red), 'Jelena' (yellow and copper) and pale yellow 'Moonlight'. Grow in acid or neutral soil well enriched with peat or leafmould. Dappled shade is recommended. Propagate by layering.

Hibiscus

Poor cousins to their tropical relatives, these are nonetheless among the most useful of late flowering shrubs, producing their large trumpet-shaped blooms in late summer/early autumn. 1.8 m (6 ft) in height and spread. Very late starting into growth, often showing no signs of life the first year after planting till early summer. 'Blue Bird' has large single blue flowers; 'Hamabo' blush pink flowers; 'Monstrosus' very large white flowers with a crimson centre and 'Woodbridge' large carmine flowers. No routine pruning needed, though old specimens can be cut right back to old wood. Layering.

Hippophae SEA BUCKTHORN

One species, *H. rhamnoides*, is grown for its silvery, willow-like leaves and enormous crops of orange berries in autumn. 3.6 by 3.6 m (12 by 12 ft). Plant one male for every three females; cross pollination is needed to achieve fruiting. Full sun. Seeds.

Hoheria NEW ZEALAND RIBBON WOODS

Beautiful shrubs producing such large quantities of almost translucent white flowers in summer that they bow the branches down. Slightly tender and best in full sun against a wall. Any soil, good on chalk. 3 by 2.4 m (10 by 8 ft). *H. glabrata* is the best, reliable in flower. No pruning. Half-ripe cuttings or layering.

Hydrangea

Valuable because they produce their spectacular heads of red, pink, blue or white flowers in late summer and autumn, the heads lasting in colour till the frosts. Good on any soil, but gross feeders. Not by any means completely hardy, they will seldom succeed in a frost pocket. They flower on the tips of the previous season's growth, and if this gets cut by frost there will be no flowers. For this reason the old flower heads should be left on through the winter, since they provide some protection. The only routine pruning needed is to remove weak growths, old gnarled unproductive wood and the old flower-heads: these operations should be carried out in mid-spring. Most people believe that hydrangeas turn blue on acid soils, but stay pink on alkaline soils. In fact life is not quite that simple. Some pink varieties will never turn blue, no matter how acid your soil. On alkaline soils hydrangeas that will blue can be blued by hoeing in alum powder round the roots in spring: conversely, blue hydrangeas can be turned pink on acid soils by applying ground limestone. There are two basic flower types: *Hortensias*, with large rounded heads composed entirely of large, sterile flowers, and *Lacecaps* which have flat heads in which not all the flowers are of the large, sterile type.

Among the best are:
Hortensias
DEEP BLUE 'Maréchal Foch', 'Hamburg'.
DEEP PINK 'Altona', 'Europa' and 'Goliath'.
RED 'Ami Pasquier'. The reds are all smaller growing than the others – 60
to 90 cm (2 to 3 ft) instead of 1.2 to 1.5 m (4 to 5 ft).
WHITE 'Mme. E. Mouillière'.
Lacecaps 'Blue Bird' – 90 cm (3 ft) – blues well. 'Lanarth White', pure
white. 'Bluewave,' very vigorous, late flowering, needs help to blue well.

One other hydrangea is well worth growing and that is *H. paniculata*
which carries huge conical heads of sterile white flowers. The variety
'Grandiflora' has even larger heads. The plant is bone hardy, and flower
heads 45 cm (18 in) long can be produced by cutting it almost to the
ground each spring and feeding it liberally. Soft cuttings from non-
flowering shoots.

Hypericum ST. JOHN'S WORT
Grown for their large rich yellow flowers produced from early summer
till mid-autumn, they will grow in any soil in full sun. The best are *H.
patulum* 1.2 by 1 m (4 by 3 ft), and its variety 'Hidcote' which is similar
but has even larger flowers. A small grower is *H. beanii* 'Gold Cup' with
deep yellow cup-shaped blooms, while a new introduction, again a small
grower, is 'Gold Penny' with yellow blooms from early summer to
autumn, followed by eye-catching red fruits. Grow in full sun and propagate from half-ripe cuttings.

Kerria JEW'S MALLOW
K. japonica is a popular and easily grown shrub with green, suckering
stems and rather orangy yellow flowers in spring. The form usually
grown is double, 'Pleniflora', which grows to 2.4 m (8 ft). Prune out
flowering shoots after flowering. Slightly tender on exposed sites.
Suckers or hardwood cuttings.

Kolkwitzia BEAUTY BUSH
One species only is grown, *K. amabilis*, which has a graceful arching habit
of growth; produces masses of small pink tubular flowers in late spring/
early summer. Even better is the variety 'Pink Cloud'. 3.6 by 3 m (12 by
10 ft). Any soil, full sun. Cut out old shoots after flowering. Half-ripe
cuttings.

Leycesteria FLOWERING NUTMEG
Attractive green stems and heads of white and claret flowers in mid- and
late summer, followed by black berries. Height 1.8 m (6 ft), spread

1.5 m (5 ft). Best in full sun. Cut out the old flowered stems to ground level in early spring. Hardwood cuttings.

Lonicera SHRUBBY HONEYSUCKLE
Every garden should have one of the winter-flowering shrubby honey-suckles for its exquisite scent. Perhaps best-known is *L. fragrantissima*, semi-evergreen with cream flowers in late winter/early spring. Height and spread at least 1.8 m (6 ft). Half-ripe or hardwood cuttings.

Magnolia
Among the most opulent of all shrubs, most magnolias are too large for small gardens. By far the most suitable is *M. stellata*, the star magnolia, which produces enormous numbers of pure white starry flowers in early and mid-spring. It is slow growing, to at least 3 by 3 m (10 by 10 ft). 'Rosea' has blooms flushed with pink, while 'Water Lily' has larger flowers than the species. *M. liliiflora* 'Nigra' produces its deep purple,

Hydrangeas are probably the most universally planted of summer flowering shrubs. The showy flowers are sterile and remain on the plant, gradually fading, for months.

tulip-shaped flowers with the new leaves during mid- and late spring and sporadically through the summer. Size is similar to *M. stellata*. The most popular of all magnolias is *M. × soulangiana* with huge goblet-shaped flowers, white, stained with purple, in mid-spring, before the new leaves appear. Height and spread at least 4.5 m (15 ft). There are several varieties that can be recommended, like 'Amabilis', virtually pure white; 'Brozzonii', with very large white and purple flowers; 'Lennei', with massive purple and cream blooms; 'Picture', purple and white; and 'Rustica Rubra', with deep rose-red flowers. Add plenty of peat or leaf-mould to the soil before planting, and mulch the plants with these materials. The site should be sheltered from cold winds. *M. × soulangiana* is often grown against a wall. Propagate by layering.

Paeonia TREE PEONY

No other shrubs can match these for the sheer size and brilliance of colouring of the flowers, which are like huge poppies, as much as 45 cm (18 in) across, single, semi-double or double, red, pink, white or bi-coloured. All are forms of *P. suffruticosa*. One nurseryman in Britain has recently started offering a range of beautiful Japanese tree peonies: named varieties in a wide range of colours. They are perfectly hardy and suitable even for northern areas. Plant in a position sheltered from early morning sun, with the graft 8 cm (3 in) below the soil. In autumn cut back any poorly ripened wood to large buds on well-ripened wood. *P. × lemoinei* is the name given to a race of mainly yellow-flowered hybrids: among the best are 'Alice Harding', enormous sulphur yellow flowers, and 'Souvenir de Maxime Cornu', coppery orange with yellow lights. All are slow-growing to about 1.5 by 1.5 m (5 by 5 ft). They have beautiful divided leaves, often pink or copper in spring, and often with a silvery bloom on them through summer. Plants are usually grafted on stock of herbaceous paeonies. Increase by seed, stratified and left out of doors until germinated, then potted on individually, or by layering.

Perovskia RUSSIAN SAGE

Neither Russian nor a sage, nonetheless an attractive late-flowering shrub. The finest is 'Blue Spire' with lavender-blue flower spikes in late summer and greyish green deeply cut foliage. 1.2 by 1 m (4 ft by 3 ft). Likes a hot sunny place and preferably sandy soil. Cut down stems to 30 to 45 cm (12 to 18 in) from the ground in mid-spring. Propagate from half-ripe cuttings.

Philadelphus MOCK ORANGE

Eternally popular shrubs with fragrant white flowers, excellent for flower arranging. All will grow easily in any soil, preferably in sun, and all flower in early summer. Among the best are 'Beauclerk', 1.8 by 1.8 m (6 by 6 ft), very large sweetly scented white flowers; 'Belle Etoile', 1.8 by 1.5 m (6 by 5 ft), exquisitely scented very large white flowers with a slight pink flush at the base of the petals; and 'Manteau d'Hermine', 1 by 1.2 (3 by 4 ft), exceptionally free-flowering with double creamy white vanilla-scented flowers. A new variety well worth considering is 'Natchez', from the United States, with large, pure white, sweetly scented flowers. Height and spread about 1.8 m (6 ft). Prune out shoots that have flowered straight after flowering. Half-ripe or hardwood cuttings.

Physocarpus
An excellent dwarf foliage shrub is *Physocarpus opulifolius* 'Dart's Gold', with brilliant golden-yellow lobed leaves all summer. Height 60 to 80 cm (2 to 2½ ft). It is hardy and adaptable but best in full sun. Propagate from semi-ripe cuttings.

Poncirus JAPANESE BITTER ORANGE
A fascinating plant that bears large white scented flowers which are followed by small, bitter oranges. 2.4 by 1.8 m (8 by 6 ft). The stout branches are armed with fearsome thorns and the twigs are green. Sun; no pruning. Seed; half-ripe cuttings.

Potentilla
The shrubby potentillas are mainly varieties of *P. fruticosa* and have yellow, white, pink, red or orange flowers like rather small dog roses. Perhaps their greatest virtue is the length of their flowering season – from late spring to mid-autumn. Among the best are 'Daydawn', pinky yellow; 'Goldfinger', large deep yellow; 'Goldstar', large yellow; 'Katherine Dykes', primrose yellow; 'Princess', pink; 'Red Ace', vermilion; 'Royal Flush', rose-pink; 'Tangerine', coppery red; and 'Tilford Cream', creamy white. Average height and spread of potentillas is 1 m (3 ft), but some are shorter. No pruning needed, except to trim off dead flowers. Best in sunny positions with well-drained soil. Easily increased from half-ripe cuttings.

Prunus
A huge family which includes the flowering cherries as well as the peaches, almonds, nectarines and the laurel. *P. tenella* is a dwarf, suckering shrub from Siberia, as hardy as they come, growing to about 1.2 m (4 ft) but spreading slowly and indefinitely, covered in spring in gay pink blossoms. The form 'Fire Hill' has bright rose red flowers. Cut out about half the old flowering shoots directly after flowering. Increase by soft cuttings. *P. triloba* has every twig of the previous season's growth covered

in icing-pink double rosette-like flowers in mid-spring. Prune hard after flowering. 1.2 by 1.5 m (4 by 5 ft). Usually sold as grafted plants – watch for suckers! Increase by layering.

Rhododendron (including azalea)
Many people do not realise that there are several deciduous rhododendrons. Then there are the deciduous azaleas, which are botanically rhododendrons. All need acid soil with a cool moist root run. Mix plenty of peat or leafmould into the soil before planting and mulch with these materials. Most do best in dappled shade, although full sun is acceptable. No pruning needed, but remove dead flower heads.

There are several deciduous or semi-evergreen rhododendron species worth considering. *R. dauricum* is semi-evergreen and has rose-purple flowers from mid-winter to early spring. The variety 'Midwinter' has reddish purple flowers. Grows to over 1.5 m (5 ft) in height.
Rhododendron mucronulatum is a slender shrub about 1.8 m (6 ft) in height with funnel-shaped, eye-catching rose-purple flowers from mid-winter to early spring. *R.* 'Praecox' is semi-evergreen, 1 to 1.5 m (3 to 5 ft) in height, with rose-purple funnel-shaped blooms in late winter/early spring.

Coming on to deciduous azaleas, *R. luteum* is the common yellow azalea with highly fragrant yellow flowers in late spring and good autumn leaf colour. Height at least 2.4 m (8 ft).

Then there are the azalea hybrids, divided into several groups:
Ghent azaleas. These flower in late spring/early summer and have a height and spread of about 1.8 m (6 ft). They have tubular, often highly scented blooms.
Mollis azaleas. These bloom in late spring and have scentless funnel-shaped flowers. The leaves display good autumn colour.
Knap Hill azaleas. These constitute a fine group, flowering in late spring/ early summer and with good autumn leaf colour. The young foliage is often flushed with bronze. Depending on variety, height and spread range from 1 to 2 m (3 to 6 ft).
Exbury azaleas. These are similar to Knap Hill azaleas and again highly recommended.

There are many named varieties in all of these groups so it is a matter of choosing the colours you prefer: they range from white, through every shade of pink and orange to brightest scarlet and crimson.

Rhus SUMACH
Rather tree-like shrubs with pinnate leaves (like those of an ash tree, but larger), grown mainly for their autumn colouring. This is best when the plants are grown in full sun on very poor soil, and the leaves turn every

The potentillas are all easily grown shrubs of neat, compact habit with a very long flowering season from late spring to mid-autumn.

possible hue of yellow, pink, orange and scarlet. The branches are very thick, somewhat hairy, and the plant takes on a rather ugly outline in winter when bare. 3.6 by 4.5 m (12 by 15 ft). The best species is *R. typhina*, the stag's horn sumach, with leaves up to 60 cm (2 ft) long. The variety 'Laciniata' has very finely cut leaves and is even better. Propagate from suckers.

Ribes FLOWERING CURRANT
Very popular easily grown shrubs, 2.4 by 2.4 m (8 by 8 ft), thriving in any soil, in sun or some shade. They produce hanging clusters of pink flowers in early spring. The colour is rather crude, the flowers smell of tom-cats and they are often grown next to forsythia, with which they clash abominably. Usually grown is *R. sanguineum*, which has rather washed-out pink flowers: much better coloured, being deep red, are 'King Edward VII' and 'Pulborough Scarlet'. Prune hard after flowering if desired. Layers or hardwood cuttings.

Romneya CALIFORNIAN TREE POPPY
One of the most lovely of all deciduous shrubs, with purest white 15 cm
(6 in) poppy-like flowers borne mid-summer to early autumn; the
flowers have a huge centre boss of fluffy golden anthers. Tends to behave
like a herbaceous perennial in colder districts. 1.8 by 1.8 m (6 by 6 ft).
Leaves poppy-like but smooth and grey-green. *R. coulteri* is the species
usually grown but there is a hybrid called 'White Cloud' which is very
vigorous and has extremely large blooms. Grow in a sunny sheltered spot
with very well drained soil, enriched with peat or leafmould. In autumn
cut down dead stems. Protect crowns of plants with bracken or straw
over winter. Once planted leave undisturbed as romneya hates root
disturbance.

Rosa ROSE
Among the best roses for today's shrub border are the modern shrub
roses and some of the species or wild roses. Of the shrub roses, ideally
choose the repeat-flowering kinds which have several flushes of bloom
during summer and autumn. Most grow between 1.5 and 2.4 m (5 and
8 ft) in height, with a similar spread. Of the many good varieties, I can
recommend 'Cardinal Hulme', deep purple, fragrant blooms; 'China-
town', deep yellow; 'Elmshorn', large clusters of small double flowers in
bright, strong pink; 'Fred Loads', large single blooms in vivid orange-
vermilion; 'Golden Wings', large, single, scented, light golden-yellow
flowers; 'Kassel', big clusters of double flowers in deep orange-red;
'Marguerite Hilling', palest pink flowers; 'Nevada', big single white
blooms, touched with pink; and 'Westerland', big clusters of semi-double
flowers in brilliant golden orange.
   The hybrid musk roses also well deserve border space for their beauti-
fully scented flowers which are produced well into the autumn. Average
height and spread is about 1.5 m (5 ft). Popular varieties include 'Corne-
lia', pink; 'Felicia', palest pink; 'Penelope', light salmon pink; and
'Prosperity', pure white.
   Modern rugosa roses well worth considering are 'Hunter' with double
bright crimson flowers in summer, repeating in autumn; and 'Kordes'
Robusta' with single, brilliant scarlet flowers. Height and spread of both
at least 1.5 m (5 ft).
   There are lots of good species or wild roses for the shrub border. Some
of my favourites include *R. moyesii*, one of the best for autumn hips,
which are flagon-shaped and bright waxy red. The single deep red
flowers are produced in summer. A well-known variety is 'Geranium'.
Both grow to about 2.4 m (8 ft) in height, with a similar spread. *R.
omeiensis pteracantha* is a fabulous rose: it has ferny foliage, large vicious

red thorns which are translucent when young, small single white flowers and red hips. Blooms in spring; height and spread about 2.4 m (8 ft).

Rosa rubrifolia is noted for its purple-grey foliage carried on deep red stems. The pink flowers are not very showy but the crops of brown-red autumn hips certainly are. This rose looks lovely planted with a purple-leaved shrub, such as cotinus. Height and spread around 1.2 m (4 ft). *R. xanthina* 'Canary Bird' produces single golden-yellow flowers in late spring and early summer and has bright green ferny foliage. Height and spread around 1.5 to 1.8 m (5 to 6 ft).

None of these roses requires any regular pruning – only the removal when necessary of any very old or dead wood. All like plenty of sun and a fertile, well-drained soil. Mulching with farmyard manure will be appreciated, as will spring and summer feeds of rose fertilizer. Cut off dead blooms.

Rubus ORNAMENTAL BRAMBLE
Some of the brambles have attractive white stems, which show up really well in winter, like *R. cockburnianus*, 2.4 by 1.8 m (8 by 6 ft). *R. thibetanus* 'Silver Fern' has ferny foliage and attains a similar size. Grow in sun or partial shade in well-drained soil and cut down stems in early spring each year. Propagate by layering.

Salix WILLOW
Several of the willows can be grown as shrubs by cutting them almost to ground level in early spring each year. They are valued for their coloured stems, which show up particularly well in winter. I can recommend *S. alba* 'Chermesina', the scarlet willow, with eye-catching orange-scarlet stems; and *S. alba* 'Vitellina', the golden willow, with bright, deep yellow bark. Willows grow particularly well in moist or wet soil and show up best in a sunny spot. Propagate from hardwood cuttings.

Sambucus ELDER
One of the most spectacular elders is *S. racemosa* 'Plumosa Aurea' with deeply cut golden-yellow foliage in summer. It is a slow grower, attaining about 1.5 m (5 ft) in height and spread. Grows in any good soil, in sun or partial shade. Propagate from half-ripe or hardwood cuttings.

Spartium SPANISH BROOM
S. junceum has rush-like stems bearing at their tips large pea-type flowers, deep yellow and wonderfully scented, from early to late summer; 2.4 by 1.8 m (8 by 6 ft). Full sun, any soil, good on chalk. Short-lived. Seed.

Spiraea
A very free-flowering, easily grown group of shrubs. The individual

flowers are small, but borne in dense heads which make them effective. The earliest to flower is *S. thunbergii*, height and spread about 1.8 m (6 ft), a twiggy bush smothered with white flowers in early and mid-spring. This is followed by *S.* × *arguta*, the foam of May or bridal wreath, of similar stature, covered in showers of white flowers all along the branches during late spring. *S. nipponica tosaensis* (also known as 'Snowmound') forms a dense mound, 1 to 1.2 m (3 to 4 ft) high and wide, smothered in white flowers during early summer. There are some excellent *S.* × *bumalda* varieties, like the dwarf 'Anthony Waterer' with flat heads of crimson flowers in mid- and late summer; and 'Goldflame' with gold foliage in spring, which later turns green. The new *S. japonica* 'Golden Princess' has bright gold foliage all summer and bright pink flowers, carried in flat heads during mid-summer. Height and spread about 60 cm (2 ft). Grow spiraeas in any good soil in a sunny spot and prune back the old flowered shoots of early-flowering kinds immediately after flowering. All stems of *S.* × *bumalda* and *S. japonica* can be cut hard back in early spring. Propagate from softwood or hardwood cuttings.

Symplocos

Only one species, *S. paniculata*, is grown. Rare but worth while. Slow growing to 2.4 by 1.8 m (8 by 6 ft). Leaves small, bright green in spring, clusters of white, hawthorn-like slightly scented flowers in early summer and brilliant turquoise berries remaining on the branches through winter. Plant two or more to obtain berries. Fruits best in a sheltered sunny position facing south or west. Needs acid soil. Seed or layering.

Syringa LILAC

Too well known to need much description, lilacs are treasured for their large pyramidal flowers as well as for their scent. What is not generally appreciated is that they are gross feeders, robbing the soil of all goodness around them and are not, therefore, the best of companions in a mixed shrub border. It is hopeless to try to underplant them with low-growing rhododendrons, for example, for these will simply die of drought and starvation. Most tend to sucker, some faster than others: digging the soil round the roots increases the rate and amount of suckering. Suckers should be removed with a sharp, upward pull. Lilacs are also large-growing, ultimately reaching 4.5 by 4.5 m (15 by 15 ft). Try to avoid buying grafted plants, as these usually sucker worse than plants on their own roots, unless they are grafted on to privet, when suckers will not be a problem. There are so many to choose from, but the following are among the best:

Single 'Charles X', long, purple-red flowers, has been popular a very long time; 'Congo', deep lilac red; 'Firmament', lilac-blue; 'Maréchal Foch', carmine-rose; 'Maud Notcutt', pure white; 'Primrose', primrose-yellow; 'Sensation', purple-red, edged white; and 'Souvenir de Louis Spaeth', deep red.

Double 'Charles Joly', deep purple-red; 'General Pershing', purple-violet; 'Katherine Havemeyer', lavender-purple; 'Madame Lemoine', pure white; 'Michael Buchner', rose-lilac; 'Mrs Edward Harding', red; 'Paul Thirion', rose pink; and 'Souvenir d'Alice Harding', white.

Another lilac well worth growing, especially in the smaller garden, is *S. palibiniana*, height and spread at least 1.8 m (6 ft), with lavender-purple blooms in late spring. To get the best out of lilacs every flower truss should be removed after flowering. This can be quite a chore on a large plant, but it is well worth while as you will get nearly twice as much flower the following year. It also pays to feed lilacs, preferably with farmyard or horse manure. This should not be placed right up against the plant, but in a ring where the branches end – for that is where the feeding roots will be. Layering or half-ripe cuttings.

Tamarix TAMARISK

Grown for their feathery appearance and for their soft green spring foliage and yellow autumn leaves, rather than for their flowers, which are a bit wishy-washy and ineffective. Never shapely, they form leggy shrubs up to 3 by 2.4 m (10 by 8 ft). Less tall and less leggy if cut annually almost to ground level. *T. tetrandra* flowers in late spring on the previous season's wood. Rather more showy are *T. pentandra* and its forms, notably 'Rubra', which flower in late summer on the current season's growth. Excellent by the sea, where they will grow in almost pure sand. Inland they need full sun and good soil. Hardwood cuttings.

Viburnum

A large genus of both deciduous and evergreen shrubs. They are so variable that anyone gardening on a chalk soil would do well to consider using them in quantity and in variety. *V. farreri* (formerly and probably better known as *V. fragrans*) is the most widely planted. Its great virtue is that it produces its pinkish, strongly almond-scented flowers throughout the winter; its great failing is that it forms a rambling great tangle of wood 3 m (10 ft) tall spreading almost indefinitely by suckers and layering itself wherever a branch touches the ground. *V.* × *bodnantense* 'Dawn' suckers less, has pink flowers in winter and is generally a better buy. *V. carlesii* is a fine spring flowering species with pink buds opening to pure white and a good scent: 1.5 by 1.8 m (5 by 6 ft). *V. carlcephalum* has larger flowers in huge bunches, but grows ultimately to 2.4 by 2.4 m (8 by 8 ft). *V. opulus*, the guelder rose, somewhat resembles a hydrangea, with an outer ring of large sterile flowers and an inner ring of small,

The viburnums are a huge genus of deciduous and evergreen species, some grown for their flowers, some for their leaves, and some for their colourful berries.

fertile flowers. The finest form is *V. opulus* 'Sterile' in which all the flowers are sterile – forming a large ball-shaped flower-head – giving it the popular name snowball tree. 3.6 by 4.5 m (12 by 15 ft). The dwarf form *V. opulus* 'Compactum' grows to only 1.5 by 1.5 m (5 by 5 ft). Both have good autumn colour, and the type plant and 'Compactum' have bright red berries in autumn. *V. plicatum* 'Mariesii' is an imposing plant with tiered branches. It produces masses of flat heads of white flowers in late spring/early summer. Height and spread at least 3 m (10 ft). Propagate by layering or half-ripe cuttings.

Weigela

Popular easily-grown shrubs with masses of trumpet-shaped flowers in various shades. Any soil, sun or a little shade. Flowers are borne all along wood of the previous season's growth and old flowered shoots should be cut out immediately after flowering. Dull leaves and little charm of habit, with the exception of *W. florida* 'Variegata' which has attractive cream and green variegated foliage, and *W. florida* 'Foliis Purpureis' whose foliage is flushed purple. A new *florida* variety is 'Rubigold' with gold and green variegated foliage and crimson flowers. Those grown primarily for flowers include 'Bristol Ruby', ruby red; 'Eva Rathke', crimson; 'Evita', a dwarf shrub with bright scarlet blooms; 'Dart's Colourdream', a new variety with an unusual mixture of cream and rose-red flowers; 'Mont Blanc', white; and 'Newport Red', bright red. Average size is 1.8 m (6 ft) in height and spread. Flowering season early summer. Propagate from half-ripe or hardwood cuttings.

CHAPTER 8

EVERGREEN SHRUBS

Evergreens differ from deciduous shrubs in more ways than simply the obvious one of retaining their leaves through winter. In the first place more sumptuous flowers are to be found among the evergreens than among the deciduous shrubs, and in the second place they provide a year-round screen for the garden. But they do have their disadvantages. Many come from warmer climates than our own, so they are not so well adapted to our cold winters as the deciduous shrubs and some of them tend to look a bit sorry for themselves by the end of winter.

The other factor that should always be borne in mind when planting them is that most also come from a rather damper climate than ours – one with higher atmospheric humidity than is found in this country. In general this is why most of the finest specimens of evergreen shrubs are to be found in the warmer, wetter western parts of the British Isles: it is also why a great many of them are grown in woodland conditions, since the atmospheric humidity in woodland is invariably higher than in open ground.

All this should not, however, discourage anyone from growing evergreens. Quite a number are completely hardy – like the native holly, *Ilex aquifolium*, and its varieties. All evergreens do best if planted in soil that has been enriched with peat or leaf-mould which help to retain moisture. Some of the others come from hot sunny climates and are best grown in sandy soil at the foot of a south or west wall.

As for effectiveness, generally speaking those with glossy leaves look less drab in winter than those with matt leaves. Variegated evergreens really come into their own in winter and again it is those with glossy leaves that look the best.

In general very few evergreens need pruning: most of them simply need dead-heading. Any pruning should be done immediately after flowering. Some will only grow on acid soil and where this is so it is mentioned in the descriptive list that follows.

Abelia
Beautiful shrubs with small leaves and tubular flowers: not spectacular, but they have a quiet charm. One species is hardy, *A.* × *grandiflora*, 1.8

by 1.2 m (6 by 4 ft), which is semi-evergreen and has pink and white flowers from mid-summer to mid-autumn. The variety 'Francis Mason' has yellow leaves and white flowers flushed pink. Prune out old branches periodically. Half-ripe cuttings. Best grown as a wall shrub.

Berberis BARBERRY

The evergreen members of this family are, in the main, fully hardy, will grow in any soil, sun or part shade, are no trouble, need no pruning and keep weeds down. Among the best are *B. darwinii*, probably best of all, 2.4 by 2.4 (8 by 8 ft), tiny, prickly dark green leaves, brilliant orange-yellow flowers in spring, bluish-purple berries in autumn. Seeds freely. *B.* × *stenophylla*, 3 by 3 m, (10 by 10 ft), has arching branches covered in deep yellow flowers during spring, followed by purple berries. There is a new variety called 'Cream Showers', with creamy white blooms. The variety 'Corallina Compacta' is useful for the front of the border, growing 30 by 60 cm (1 by 2 ft), with rich golden flowers. *B. verruculosa*, 1.2 by 1.2 m (4 by 4 ft), arching branches wreathed in very thickly set dark green leaves, white beneath, clusters of drooping golden-yellow flowers in late spring, followed by black fruits covered with a blue bloom in autumn: some of the foliage turns crimson in autumn – unusual among evergreens. *B. buxifolia* 'Nana' is another dwarf, 60 by 60 cm (2 by 2 ft), yellow flowers in spring and purplish winter foliage. Half-ripe cuttings are slow to root; seed is easy.

Camellia

Strictly for acid soils, camellias are among the most glamorous of all shrubs: they have a quality and dignity about them that few shrubs can rival. Anyone with an alkaline soil can grow them in tubs of lime-free compost: the compost should be watered only with rain water from a butt, never with tap water. In winter the tubs should be wrapped with fibre-glass or straw, covered with polythene, to keep the frost out. Camellias should always be planted in a situation where they are shaded from the early morning sun: it is not frost that destroys their flower buds, but rapid thawing. If planted out of reach of early morning sun the thawing will be gradual and will do less damage; the north or west side of a shrub or building is ideal.

Essentially forest undershrubs, camellias must have some shade during part of the day: too much sun scorches the foliage – too much shade and they will not flower freely. They need more sun in the north of the country than in the south. Most of those mentioned here are fully hardy, but should be protected with a hessian screen from north or east winds for their first two or three winters.

Slow-growing, they ultimately form very large plants, at least 4.5 by

The varieties of *Camellia* × *williamsii*, such as 'Inspiration', are superb, hardy garden shrubs, producing masses of flowers between autumn and spring, depending on variety. Site them where their blooms are sheltered from cold winds.

3.6 m (15 by 12 ft) – but that takes a life-time. If you move house, always take your favourite camellias with you: they move well.

The sorts usually grown are cultivars of *Camellia japonica*, which has dark green glossy leaves. The flowers can be single, semi-double or fully double and vary considerably in form. Colours range from white through pinks to scarlet and crimson, with bi-colours as well. There are hundreds of named varieties, but the naming is somewhat confused. In general few garden centres carry more than a dozen or so varieties, but these are usually among the most popular. Pure whites are generally best avoided: they are too easily browned by frosts. Some of the best are 'Contessa Lavinia Maggi', white, striped and splashed crimson, pointed petals; occasionally sports pure pink flowers. 'Adolphe Audusson', semi-double bright scarlet with a large boss of yellow stamens. 'Mars' is very similar. 'Jupiter', large single of bright scarlet with a good centre. 'Mrs. D. W. Davies', huge cup-shaped flowers of pale blush pink with a broad central mass of stamens: has tremendous quality. 'Drama Girl', slightly more tender than most and best against a west wall, has the largest flowers of all hardy camellias, brightest carmine. 'Lady Clare', one of the best pinks, with a graceful weeping habit, very large flowers. 'Furoan', medium-sized pink flowers with a good centre; very pleasing. 'Betty Sheffield Supreme', large flowers, white with a pink picotee edge; superb. 'Elegans', formal semi-double pink, probably the most widely planted of all camellias. 'Donckelarii', very large semi-double with white streaks. 'Grand Slam', huge double deep red.

C. saluenensis is a smaller growing species with matt, net-veined leaves and pure pink single flowers. Very lovely but less well known; detests cold winds, though withstands frosts well. This has been crossed with *C. japonica* to produce a race known as *C.* × *williamsii*, the best of which is 'Donation' – probably the finest camellia ever raised: tall, narrow habit, small matt leaves and large semi-double flowers of a vibrant yet soft pink shot with darker veins; very spectacular; flowers when very small. 'Anticipation', deep rose, 'Debbie', pink, 'Francis Hanger', white, 'J. C. Williams', bright pink, and 'St. Ewe', rose pink, are other *williamsii* varieties that can be recommended.

Camellias flower mainly between mid-winter and late spring, depending on the weather. Add plenty of peat or leafmould to the soil before planting, keep well watered in dry periods and mulch with peat or leafmould. Propagate by layering.

Ceanothus CALIFORNIAN LILAC
The finest ceanothus, those with the purest and brightest blue flowers, all belong here. They are rather more tender than the deciduous species and

best grown against a sunny wall. The flowers are individually tiny but borne in dense spikes produced in great quantities. They should be planted very young from pots and never moved once planted. Any soil. Prune only to keep reasonably close to the wall, removing as little growth as possible. Plant in spring. Among the best are *C. rigidus*, the earliest to flower, early spring onwards, rich indigo-blue flowers, cotoneaster-like leaves, glossy. *C. dentatus* and its forms flower in late spring; the best is 'Floribundus', with powder-blue flowers. *C.* 'Cascade' is a wonderful mid-blue with a slightly weeping habit, very free flowering. All reach about 3 by 2.4 m (10 by 8 ft), except 'Cascade' which is smaller growing. *C. thyrsiflorus repens* is quite different, having a creeping habit and forming a large, low mound about 1.8 m (6 ft) across; it is much hardier than the other evergreen species, makes good ground cover and has sky-blue flowers. Half-ripe cuttings.

Choisya MEXICAN ORANGE BLOSSOM
One species, *C. ternata*, 1.8 by 2.4 m (6 by 8 ft), needs a position sheltered by other shrubs or by a wall, is best with a little shade since full sun makes the leaves yellow, and will grow in any soil. Leaves bright polished mid-green, darker in shade, lighter in sun, very aromatic when crushed, masses of waxy white starry flowers in late spring and then sporadically through the year, with a tremendous perfume. Any growths damaged by frost can be cut out. A new variety called 'Sundance' has bright golden foliage throughout the year and scented white flowers. It's a slow grower to 90 cm (3 ft). Propagation by half-ripe cuttings.

Cistus SUN ROSE
Delightful shrubs with pointed, leathery leaves which give off a pungent aroma in damp weather and large, single rose-like flowers, usually white or pink, often with good markings in the centre, opening in great numbers each day but fading again by late afternoon, flowering through mid-summer. Excellent companions for heathers and brooms. Any soil, but especially useful on poor soils. Full sun. In cold districts best against a wall. None is very long-lived – 10 years or so – and none is very hardy. Among the best are *C × corbariensis*, 1.5 by 1.5 m (5 by 5 ft), rosy-pink buds, white flowers with a yellow flush; one of the hardiest; red stems. *C. × cyprius*, 1.8 by 1.8 m (6 by 6 ft), white flowers with a maroon blotch at the base of the petals, sage green leaves. *C × purpureus*, 1.2 by 1.2 m (4 by 4 ft), very large flowers, purple-red with deep black-red blotches. One of the most popular cistus is 'Silver Pink', 90 cm (3 ft) in height and spread, with silvery pink flowers and very hardy. Remove any wood damaged by frost. Half-ripe cuttings.

One of the best heathers for foliage colour is *Calluna vulgaris* 'Gold Haze'. Like all varieties of ling, it needs to be grown in acid or lime-free soil.

Cotoneaster

The evergreen species embrace a range of plants from prostrate crawlers to small trees. Flowers often pass unnoticed, but the berries are usually conspicuous: they are also liked by birds. One of the lowest growing is *C. dammeri radicans*, spreading indefinitely, fully weed-proof, rooting as it grows, glossy leaves, white flowers, very large red berries. *C. microphyllus* has tiny, glossy leaves and a low mounding habit, but spreading, the branch ends rooting; white flowers, scarlet berries. Of the taller-growing species *C. franchetii* is one of the best, 3 by 3 m (10 by 10 ft), grey-green oval leaves, and small orange-red berries in great quantities. Very large shrubs, attaining over 3 m (10 ft) in height and spread, are 'Cornubia' with heavy crops of red berries, and 'Exburiensis' with yellow fruits. Propagate from semi-ripe cuttings.

Daphne

D. odora 'Aureomarginata' is an attractive shrub with cream-edged leaves and pale purplish flowers from mid-winter to mid-spring. Height and spread about 1.8 m (6 ft). Good on chalk soils; sun or partial shade. Half-ripe cuttings.

Desfontainea CHILEAN HOLLY

One species grown, *D. spinosa*, a slightly tender evergreen with small, holly-like leaves and tubular scarlet and yellow flowers borne from mid- to late summer. Very slow growing but ultimately 1.8 by 1.5 m (6 by 5 ft). The form 'Harold Comber' has large flowers. Acid soil, plenty of peat or leaf-mould mixed in. Flowers best in a cool position in partial shade. Seed; half-ripe cuttings; layers.

Elaeagnus
E. pungens 'Maculata' is one of the brighest of all variegated shrubs. Leaves oval, pointed, the centre bright daffodil gold, surrounded by a lighter yellow, streaks of pale green and a dark green margin. Really comes into its own in winter sunshine. Flowers insignificant but strongly scented, autumn. Also worth considering are two *E.* × *ebbingei* varieties: 'Gilt Edge' with yellow-edged leaves, and 'Limelight' whose leaves are blotched gold in the centre. Any soil; sun. Cut out any green-leaved shoots. 3 by 3 m (10 by 10 ft) but slow growing. Half-ripe cuttings, slow to root.

Embothrium CHILEAN FIRE BUSH
Probably the most brilliantly coloured of all flowering shrubs that can be grown out of doors in the British Isles, an established plant is breath-taking. Generally regarded as tender, but people seem to be realizing at last that one form is virtually hardy in all but the bleakest gardens. This is *E. coccineum lanceolatum* 'Norquinco Valley' which is semi-evergreen and has lost most of its leaves by the end of winter. Flowers tubular, 5 cm (2 in) long, produced in clusters all around and all along the young branches, being borne in such quantities that they literally hide the branch; brightest orange-scarlet; early summer. Plant very young from pots in acid soil with plenty of peat and/or leaf-mould mixed in. Pinch out growing tip to keep bushy: never prune. Grows rapidly for about three years to 1.8 m (6 ft) then settles down to flowering and grows more slowly. Ultimately 6 m (20 ft) tall, but narrow in habit. Tends to sucker slowly: these should be carefully removed for increase; alterna-tively increase by seed. *Never* disturb the roots; plant ground cover around it when newly planted and let this keep the weeds down.

Escallonia
Quick-growing summer and early autumn evergreen or semi-evergreen shrubs with small flowers borne in huge quantities. Leaves very dark, glossy, small. Any soil; sun. Do very well near the sea; need the shelter of a wall or other shrubs in cold districts. Among the best are 'Apple Blossom', pink and white; 'C. F. Ball', crimson; 'Donard Beauty', rose-red; 'Donard Brilliance', rose-red; 'Donard Seedling', white; 'Peach Blossom', peach pink; 'Pride of Donard', rose-pink; and 'Slieve Donard', apple-blossom pink. All are medium-sized shrubs, approximately 1.8 m (6 ft) in height and spread. A promising new variety is 'Red Elf' with brilliant crimson-red flowers, height up to 1.2 m (4 ft). Propagate from half-ripe cuttings.

Eucryphia
The evergreen eucryphias need an acid or neutral soil with plenty of peat and/or leaf-mould added, are rather tender when young but quite hardy once established and so spectacular that they should be tried wherever conditions suit. The best is *E. × nymansensis* 'Nymansay', which forms a narrow column 4.5 to 6 m (15 to 20 ft) tall but seldom more than 2.4 m (8 ft) wide and bears in late summer large white flowers that smother the whole plant. Fast growing. Roots should be shaded with paving stones when young, with ground-cover plants when established. Flowers best in sun; prefers shelter from cold winds. Layers; half-ripe cuttings – rather slow to root.

Euonymus
Several of the *E. fortunei* varieties make excellent evergreen ground cover, including 'Emerald 'n' Gold', bushy habit, gold-variegated leaves; 'Emerald Gaiety', upright spreading habit, leaves edged with white; and 'Variegatus', greyish, white-edged leaves, trailing habit. The varieties of *E. japonicus* form large shrubs, at least 3 m (10 ft) in height and 1.8 m (6 ft) in width. Some are attractively variegated, like 'Aureopictus', green and gold; 'Macrophyllus Albus', white and green; and 'Ovatus Aureus', cream and green. All the euonymus are very adaptable as regards soils and situation, being ideal for shade. Half-ripe cuttings.

Fatsia FALSE CASTOR-OIL PLANT
F. japonica is a foliage shrub with huge maple-like glossy evergreen leaves and thick stems. Any soil. Leaves look best in shade when they turn a very dark green; lighter green in sun. Flowers white in curious ball-shaped clusters in late autumn. About 2.4 by 2.4 m (8 by 8 ft) – slow-growing. Seed; half-ripe cuttings.

× *Fatshedera lizei*
A hybrid of *Fatsia japonica* and the common ivy. Forms a sprawling shrub about 90 cm (3 ft) but spreading indefinitely with fine, maple-like leaves of glossy green, making excellent ground cover for shade. Looks lovely with *Tropaeolum speciosum* growing through it. Half-ripe cuttings.

Garrya elliptica TASSEL BUSH
Californian evergreen with dull grey-green leaves grown for its pale greyish catkins produced in late winter/early spring. Fast growing to 3 by 2.4 m (10 by 8 ft). Best as a wall-shrub on any aspect; if grown in the open needs the shelter of other shrubs. Male plants have better catkins than female plants, normally 15 cm (6 in) long. The selected form 'James Roof' has even longer catkins. Any soil. No routine pruning. Half-ripe cuttings or layers. Plant from pots and do not transplant.

Gaultheria
Useful berrying shrubs for acid, moist, peaty soil in partial shade. The checker-berry, *G. procumbens*, is useful ground cover as it is prostrate in habit, and bright red berries. Spreads to over 90 cm (3 ft). *G. shallon*, 1.8 by 1.8 m (6 by 6 ft), is very vigorous and bears deep purple berries. Propagate from half-ripe cuttings.

Halimium
Closely related to *Cistus* but usually has yellow flowers. Likes a hot, dry position in full sun. Moderately hardy, but likely to be lost in a severe winter. Usually grown is *H. lasianthum* with small grey leaves and bright yellow flowers with a maroon blotch at the base of each petal. *H. ocymoides* is very similar. Half-ripe cuttings.

HEATHERS
These are grouped together here for convenience, though botanically they belong to three genera, *Erica*, *Calluna* and *Daboecia*. They are in the main low-growing, lime-hating plants – though there are one or two taller species and some will grow on lime (see below). They make superb ground-cover plants, absolutely weed-proof, and most simply need a light trim over with garden shears after flowering to keep them tidy. They look good at the front of the border, or when grown on their own in island beds, mixed with a few dwarf conifers. They flower best in full sun. Dig in plenty of peat or leaf-mould before planting; plant close to get good ground cover; make sure the ground is completely weed-free before planting.

Heathers for lime Heathers which grow in limy or chalky soils include *Erica herbacea (E. carnea)*, *E. erigena (E. mediterranea)*, *E. × darleyensis* and *E. terminalis (E. stricta)*.

Winter/Spring flowering heathers *Erica herbacea*, 30 cm (12 in), flowers mid-winter to mid-spring. 'Aurea' has golden foliage and deep pink flowers; 'King George', carmine flowers with brown tips; 'Springwood White', the best white, with showy chocolate-brown anthers; 'Springwood Pink' similar but rose-pink; 'Vivellii is the deepest red heather, its leaves turning dark bronze in winter. *E. erigena* is taller growing to 90 cm (3 ft), gets cut back in hard winters but normally recovers, flowers smaller, pink, spring. The above two have been crossed to produce *E. × darleyensis*, 45 cm (18 in). 'A. T. Johnson', free-flowering deep magenta; 'J. H. Brummage', pink flowers, golden foliage; 'Silberschmelze', white flowers.

Summer/Autumn flowering heathers *Daboecia*, 60 cm (2 ft), bell-shaped flowers in drooping clusters. *D. cantabrica* 'Alba' has white flowers; 'Atropurpurea', deep pink flowers. *Erica cinerea* 'Golden Drop' is grown for its coppery-golden foliage which turns rusty red in winter, seldom flowers, but very effective. *E. tetralix*, the native cross-leaved heath; 'Con Underwood' is the best form, grey-green mounds with crimson flowers. *Calluna vulgaris*, the common native heath, also known as Scottish heather or Ling; 'Alba Plena' has double white flowers; 'County Wicklow', double pink flowers; 'Gold Haze', foliage purest gold all the year, flowers white; 'Goldsworth Crimson', deep crimson flowers; 'H. E. Beale', still one of the best, double pink flowers. *Erica terminalis*, 2.4 by 1.2 m (8 by 4 ft), pink flowers which turn russet and look good all winter; does best on lime. Mound-layering is the easiest means of increase: just pile sandy soil over the crown of the plant and it will root into this; lift and divide in autumn. Half-ripe cuttings.

Hebe SHRUBBY VERONICA
A variable genus, some good in flower (mostly rather tender and best in coastal districts); some resembling conifers and some making good ground cover.
For Flowers These are mainly tender. Take half-ripe cuttings to ensure against losses. Flowers in terminal spikes. Among the best are 'Autumn Glory', small, purplish leaves, purple flowers, blooms most of the summer and autumn; 'Great Orme', long spikes of deep pink flowers, narrow, willow-like leaves; *H.* × *andersonii* 'Variegata', cream and pale green leaves, very effective, deep lavender flowers; 'Simon Delaux', carmine flowers, and 'Midsummer Beauty', lavender blooms in long spikes, pale green foliage. All grow about 1.2 m (4 ft) in height and spread.
Conifer-like *H. armstrongii*, whipcord foliage in deep yellow-green, 90 by 90 cm (3 by 3 ft); *H. cupressoides*, similar stature, greyish-green foliage.
Ground cover There is a really outstanding plant here: *H. pinguifolia* 'Pagei', 15 by 90 cm (6 by 36 in), with small, rounded, blue-grey leaves and white flowers. 'Emerald Green' has bright green foliage and grows 30 to 45 cm (12 to 18 in) in height and spread. Of similar stature is *H. rakaiensis (H. subalpina)*, with light green foliage and white flowers.
Propagate hebes from half-ripe cuttings and grow in well-drained soil and full sun.

Helianthemum ROCK ROSE
Mat-forming shrubs with small oval leaves and richly coloured single-rose-like flowers. Hot dry positions. Single-flowered types are most charming, but the flowers are very short-lived. Double-flowered types

The sheep's laurel or calico bush, *Kalmia latifolia*, is closely related to rhododendrons. It needs the same sort of soil but will stand more sun.

hold their flowers for three or four days, instead of one day only, and have a much longer flowering season. Early and mid-summer. Trim over with shears after flowering to keep neat. Dozens of named varieties in every shade of red, yellow, pink, orange and white; some have variegated foliage. Select as available. Half-ripe cuttings.

Helichrysum CURRY PLANT
H. angustifolium is grown for its grey lavender-like foliage topped with sprays of yellow flowers in summer. Plant in spring. Full sun, best on sandy soils. Gets a bit tatty after four or five years; cut back to old wood. Half-ripe cuttings.

Hypericum ST. JOHN'S WORT
The most useful member of this genus is the ubiquitous *H. calycinum*, also known as the rose of Sharon, growing to 45 cm (18 in), bright brown stems and large bright yellow flowers; it makes excellent ground cover in full sun, slightly less good in shade, flowers all summer and autumn. Needing more sun, but also good as ground cover, is *H. moserianum*, 75 by 120 cm (2½ by 4 ft), again with large yellow flowers all summer and into autumn. The variety 'Tricolor' has green, white and pink variegated leaves. Propagate *calycinum* by division; *moserianum* from half-ripe cuttings.

Ilex HOLLY
Most of the hollies ultimately form very tall shrubs indeed, but are slow growing. All the following are forms of the native holly, *I. aquifolium*. Females carry the berries, and need a male to pollinate them, unless otherwise stated. 'Argentea Marginata', broad, silver-margined leaves, bushy habit, free-fruiting; 'Golden King', leaves green with a bright gold margin and few spines, female; 'Pyramidalis', dense growth, very free fruiting, self-fertile; 'Argentea Pendula' (Perry's weeping silver holly), a gracefully weeping holly with silver-margined leaves, very free fruiting; 'J. C. van Tol', masses of berries, virtually spineless leaves; 'Bacciflava', heavy crops of bright yellow berries; 'Ferox Argentea', male, the silver hedgehog holly with white variegated leaves, very prickly. Also worth considering is *Ilex crenata* 'Golden Gem', a dwarf spreading shrub used as ground cover with small yellow leaves. Cut out any branches that produce entirely green leaves – otherwise no pruning. Half-ripe cuttings, very slow to root; layers when convenient.

Kalmia CALICO BUSH
Closely related to rhododendrons; and also needing acid soil containing plenty of peat or leaf-mould. Will withstand more sun than rhododendrons. Best known is *K. latifolia*, 2.4 by 2.4 m (8 by 8 ft) with flat heads

of neat pentagonal pink flowers with deeper pink spots; 'Clementine Churchill' has deeper pink flowers. Seedlings are variable in depth of colour. *K. angustifolia*, 1.2 by 1.2 m (4 by 4 ft), forms a dense, slowly suckering shrub with deep pink flowers and bronze winter foliage, useful at the front of a border. 'Rubra' has deeper pink flowers. Seed; layering.

Lavandula LAVENDER

Always popular, this does best on light, sandy soil in full sun. Grey leaves, spikes of strongly scented lavender flowers. All parts of the shrub are aromatic. Old English lavender is *L. angustifolia* (*L. spica*), height and spread 1 to 1.2 m (3 to 4 ft), flowering mid- to late summer. Good varieties are 'Grappenhall', 'Hidcote', 'Munstead' and 'Vera' (commonly known as Dutch lavender). Trim over with shears to keep neat. Old leggy plants should be thrown out and new ones planted. Cuttings root easily at any season. Seed is easy, but seedlings vary in colour and vigour.

Leucothoe

A colourful ground-cover plant for acid soils is *L. fontanesiana* 'Rainbow' whose leaves are variegated cream, yellow and pink. White flowers in summer. Height 60 cm (2 ft). Can trim over after flowering to ensure dense growth. Takes sun or partial shade. Half-ripe cuttings or layering.

Lupinus TREE LUPIN

L. arboreus is a short-lived shrub to about 1.2 by 1.2 m (4 by 4 ft), fresh green trifoliate leaves and pale yellow or whitish lupin flowers in summer, scented. Good varieties are 'Golden Spire', with deep yellow blooms, and the white-flowered 'Snow Queen'. Dead-head but do not prune. Good temporary gap-fillers, but little permanent use. Seed or half-ripe cuttings.

Mahonia

Attractive and useful evergreens with spine-edged pinnate leaves and clusters of yellow lily-of-the-valley like flowers in winter or early spring. The commonest is *M. aquifolium*, 1 by 1.2 m (3 by 4 ft), yellow flowers in spring followed by black berries with a blue bloom; some of the leaves turn claret in winter. Forms a dense, slowly suckering shrub making excellent ground cover in sun or shade; will grow in dense shade. 'Atropurpurea' has purple foliage. Larger, more stately mahonias, attaining a height and spread of around 2.4 m (8 ft), include *M. bealei*, flowering in winter; 'Charity', huge racemes of fragrant flowers in autumn/early winter; *M. japonica*, long pendulous racemes of bright yellow flowers from late autumn to early spring. Plant in sun or partial shade with moist soil. *M. aquifolium* can be pruned hard back in mid-spring to keep it low, if grown as ground cover. Half-ripe cuttings.

Osmanthus
One species, *O. delavayi*, 2.4 by 2.4 m (8 by 8 ft), is outstanding; tiny deep green leaves and masses of tubular, white, sweetly scented flowers in mid-spring. Highly effective. Any soil, full sun, some wall or shrub shelter in cold districts. Layers; half-ripe cuttings – but very slow to root.

× *Osmarea*
Similar to osmanthus. It is a hybrid plant, one of the parents being *Osmanthus delavayi*. Its full name is × *Osmarea burkwoodii*.

Pernettya
Superb evergreen ground-cover shrubs strictly for acid soil, producing masses of brightly coloured berries which last all through winter. *P. mucronata* is the species usually grown, or rather its varieties. Male and female plants must be planted to ensure berries. Good varieties are 'Bell's Seedling', deep red berries; 'Cherry Ripe', cherry red; and 'Pink Pearl', lilac-pink. 'Thymifolia' is a male form, useful for pollinating the females. Best in full sun, but takes semi-shade. Best to propagate by layering.

Phormium NEW ZEALAND FLAX
Grown for their erect sword-like leaves rather than their flowers which are curious but not lovely. Hardier than is generally realized, they seem to suffer more from damp, mild winters than hard ones. *P. tenax*, clump forming to 2.4 m (8 ft), leaves green; 'Purpureum', smaller growing, leaves deepest bronze-purple; 'Variegatum', leaves with a creamy white margin. There are several fairly new varieties of *P. tenax*, which make much smaller plants, including 'Maori Sunrise', pink and bronze foliage; 'Sundowner', cream, pink and purplish; and 'Yellow Wave', yellow and green. *P. cookianum* 'Cream Delight' with cream and green foliage is also a small grower. Plant phormiums in very well-drained soil, in a sheltered sunny spot. Propagate by division.

Photinia
An evergreen which has become very popular in recent years is *Photinia* × *fraseri* 'Red Robin'. This has brilliant red young leaves and is a good substitute for the red-leaved pieris, if you have an alkaline soil. Grows in sun or partial shade. Height and spread at least 3 m (10 ft). Half-ripe cuttings or layering.

Pieris
Strictly for acid soils and partial shade: very spectacular. Flowers white, bell-shaped, produced in clusters like lily-of-the-valley. One of the most spectacular is 'Forest Flame' whose young leaves are brilliant red; about 3 m (10 ft) in height and spread. Equally spectacular are varieties of *P.*

Pieris formosa forrestii is at its most spectacular in spring, with brilliant red young foliage and trusses of slightly scented white flowers.

formosa, height and spread at least 3 m (10 ft), like *forrestii* and 'Wake-hurst', with brilliant red young foliage. There are lots of good *P. japonica* varieties, height and spread up to 3 m (10 ft), including 'Blush', palest pink flowers; 'Christmas Cheer', winter blooms, flushed deep pink; 'Purity', large pure white flowers; and 'Variegata', with cream-edged leaves. Two new dwarf *japonica* varieties are 'Little Heath Green' with green foliage, and 'Little Heath' with cream-variegated foliage. These two apparently do not flower; they grow to at least 50 cm (20 in) in height and spread. Plant pieris in soil well supplied with peat or leafmould and mulch them with these. Propagate by layering.

Piptanthus EVERGREEN LABURNUM
P. laburnifolius is not too hardy and best grown in a sheltered, sunny position with well-drained soil, ideally on a south or west wall. Its young leaves are covered with silvery hairs and in late spring it produces deep yellow laburnum-like flowers. Propagate from seeds.

Pittosporum
P. tenuifolium is also on the tender side and best grown only in mild parts of the country. It has attractive light green leaves and black twigs. Height 4.5 m (15 ft), spread 2.4 m (8 ft). Good varieties include purple-leaved 'Purpureum', silvery grey 'Silver Queen' and white-edged 'Variegatum'. Grow in a sheltered, sunny spot and well-drained soil. Propagate from half-ripe cuttings.

Prunus LAUREL
Most of the laurels, *Prunus laurocerasus* varieties, are generally grown as hedging plants. However, one that makes an excellent specimen shrub is 'Marbled White', a slow grower of conical habit, over 3 m (10 ft) in height, with white and grey-green variegated leaves. Excellent for ground cover is the dwarf 'Otto Luyken', a dome-shaped plant with masses of white flowers in spring. The variegated Portugal laurel, *P. lusitanica* 'Variegata', makes a superb specimen shrub, reaching over 3 m (10 ft) in height. The leaves are conspicuously edged with white. An excellent plant for chalky soils and exposed gardens. *P. laurocerasus* is better on acid soils with shelter from cold winds. Half-ripe cuttings.

Pyracantha FIRETHORN
Usually seen as wall shrubs and ideal for clothing a north or east wall, these will also grow well in the open garden; perfectly hardy. Grown for the enormous crops of berries in autumn and winter. There are lots of pyracanthas to choose from and most make large shrubs, at least 3 m (10 ft) in height and spread. I can recommend *P. angustifolia*, orange-yellow berries; *P. atalantioides,* scarlet; *P. a.* 'Buttercup', deep yellow; *P.*

coccinea 'Lalandei', orange-red; 'Golden Charmer', orange-yellow; 'Mohave', orange-red; 'Orange Charmer', deep orange; 'Orange Glow', vivid orange-red; and *P. rogersiana* 'Flava', brilliant yellow. Very different in habit is 'Alexander Pendula', a prostrate variety which makes excellent ground cover. It has coral-red berries and can spread to at least 2 m (6 ft). If necessary, prune to restrict size after flowering, but not too hard or you will lose berries. Propagate from half-ripe cuttings.

Rhododendron

A huge genus of shrubs needing acid soil and partial shade. There are over 500 hardy species and several thousand hybrids. Enthusiasts should consult specialist books. Only the briefest selection can be given here. All need a moist soil enriched with peat or leaf-mould.

The majority of plants offered, especially by garden centres, are known as 'hardy hybrids'. The two best-sellers are 'Pink Pearl', a large growing rhododendron with huge candy-floss pink flowers, and 'Britannia', with a rather spreading habit and crimson flowers. Other good reds are 'Cynthia', Doncaster', and 'Lord Roberts'. The best of the pinks include 'Betty Wormald', coral pink with a striking deep chocolate blotch; 'Gomer Waterer', blush pink with a yellow eye; and 'Alice'. The best purples include 'Blue Peter'; 'Fastuosum Flore Pleno', a double purple; and 'Purple Splendour', rich purple with black markings. Good whites include 'Sappho', pure white with a striking dark eye; and 'Cunningham's White', earlier than most, pure white, spotted.

Apart from the hardy hybrids there are a number of very exciting newer hybrids, many of them not looking at all like the traditional old hardy hybrids. Some of the best are 'St Tudy', with willowy leaves and pure blue flowers in enormous profusion; 'Lady Chamberlain', with dangling orange bells and bluish spring foliage and 'Temple Belle' with round leaves and tubby little pink flowers early in the year. These need more shade than hardy hybrids.

There are a number of very useful dwarf rhododendrons, some of the most easily obtainable of which are 'Blue Diamond', the brightest and purest blue of the small-leaved blue hybrids; 'Elizabeth', a small, beehive-shaped shrub with medium-sized leaves and huge bright red flowers.

There are one or two other really worthwhile rhododendrons that may not be quite so easy to obtain: 'Fabia' is one of the best of these, a dwarf hybrid with brilliant orange flowers; 'Crest' is the finest of all the large-growing yellows; while 'Remo' is the finest of the dwarf yellows. *R. augustinii* is, in its finest forms, the bluest of all rhododendrons, though it may not look like a rhododendron to the uninitiated. Very variable from seed, so select a plant in flower at a nursery; poor seedlings have purple or grey flowers. For lovers of the unusual *R. serotinum* is a species with sage-green leaves that produces its scented, white, pink-tinted flowers in late summer.

One of the truly great dwarf rhododendrons is *R. yakushimanum*, with a height and spread of about 60 cm (2 ft). It is a dome-shaped plant with deep green leaves, covered beneath with fawn 'felt', and white bell-shaped flowers from pink buds in late spring. A wide range of named *yakushimanum* hybrids is available in many different colours and these are highly recommended for the small garden.

Also ideal for the small garden are the evergreen hybrid azaleas, with a height and spread of around 90 cm (3 ft). They flower profusely in late spring/early summer and are best sheltered from cold drying winds and given a position in dappled shade. There are various groups, like the famous Kurume hybrids. There is a wide range of flower colours – shades of pink, red, salmon, purple, white, etc. Choose colours that appeal to you. Among the most popular Kurume hybrids are 'Hinomayo', clear pink, and 'Hinodegiri', crimson.

Rosmarinus ROSEMARY
Aromatic shrub whose leaves have culinary uses, it is grown mainly for its grey-green foliage, the aroma it gives off in hot weather and hardly at all for its insignificant bluish flowers. The common rosemary is *R. officinalis*, height and spread about 1.8 m (6 ft); better is the variety 'Fastigiatus' (Miss Jessop's Variety), with a more erect habit. Provide a sunny sheltered spot with very well drained soil. Prune in mid-spring to maintain tidy habit. Half-ripe cuttings.

Ruta RUE
R. graveolens is grown for its charmingly divided blue-green foliage; 60 cm (2 ft), spreading slowly. Better is the shorter, more compact variety 'Jackman's Blue', with even bluer foliage. Cut hard back in spring to keep tidy. Sun; any soil. Half-ripe cuttings.

Santolina COTTON LAVENDER
Low-growing shrubs with good grey foliage. *S. chamaecyparissus*, 60 by 60 cm (2 by 2 ft), has a dense, neat habit, saw-edged leaves and yellow daisy-type flowers in summer. Best in a light sandy soil. Cut hard back each spring to keep neat, otherwise becomes straggly. Half-ripe cuttings.

Sarcococca CHRISTMAS BOX
Useful ground-cover plants for grouping in the shade. The best is *S. humilis*, a little plant 60 by 90 cm (2 by 3 ft), with narrow dark green leaves and small white strongly scented flowers in late winter. Any soil; sun or shade. Suckers; division.

Senecio

Grey-leaved shrubs, particularly useful for seaside gardens. They like plenty of sun and very well-drained soil. *Senecio* 'Sunshine' is the best known, with yellow daisy flowers in summer. Similar is *S. laxifolius*. Both are small growing shrubs. Old plants can be cut back in spring to induce a more compact habit. Propagate from half-ripe cuttings.

Skimmia

Neat berry-bearing evergreens with oval, glossy leaves, rather slow growing. Both males and females need to be planted to obtain berries. The best is *S. japonica*, the female bearing glowing red berries that do not seem to be much liked by birds and last all winter. Good varieties are 'Foremanii', female; 'Fragrans', male, with highly scented white flowers; 'Nymans', female; and 'Rubella', male, with white flowers from red buds. *S. reevesiana* has both male and female flowers on the same plant and produces good crops of crimson berries. Skimmias are not too happy on chalky soils. Withstand shade or sun. Propagate from half-ripe cuttings.

Stranvaesia

This is a cotoneaster-like shrub grown for its crops of autumn berries which are left alone by birds. The one usually grown is *S. davidiana*, height and spread at least 6 m (20 ft), with crimson berries. 'Fructuluteo' has yellow berries. Grows in any soil, sun or shade. Seeds or layering.

Viburnum

Three evergreen viburnums are well worth growing. The first is a large bush, to 3.6 by 3.6 m (12 by 12 ft), with large deep green leaves, large flat clusters of whitish flowers in early summer and large clusters of red berries in winter, known as *V. rhytidophyllum*. *V. davidii* is a dense spreading shrub 1 by 1.5 m (3 by 5 ft) at the most, with polished oval leaves with deep linear veins; flowers insignificant, but the female bears brilliant turquoise berries all through winter; plant one male to every three females. Best when grouped closely. The laurustinus, or *V. tinus*, is a highly popular shrub valued for its heads of white flowers between late autumn and late spring. Height at least 3 m (10 ft), spread at least 2.4 m (8 ft). The variety 'Eve Price' has attractive light red flower buds and pink-flushed flowers. Not quite so large as the species. The viburnums grow well in sun or partial shade and any well-drained soil – especially good on chalk. Propagate from half-ripe cuttings.

Vinca PERIWINKLE

Usually included among shrubs, though not particularly shrubby. All make dense ground cover, even in shade, though they flower best in full sun. The lesser periwinkle, *V. minor*, has small blue starry flowers from spring till frosts. There are many forms: 'Aureovariegata' has bright golden variegation; 'Variegata' has silver variegation; 'Bowles' Variety' is the deepest blue; 'Gertrude Jekyll' has white flowers; 'Atropurpurea' has reddish purple flowers; then there's the double blue 'Azurea Flore Pleno' and double purple 'Multiplex'. *V. major* is altogether a larger plant, both in leaf and flower; it flowers mainly in spring producing a few flowers sporadically through the rest of the year. Flowers bright blue. Variety 'Variegata' has cream-variegated foliage and is a far more attractive plant. Trim over with shears to keep neat. Increase by division.

Yucca

Striking plants with usually rigid sword-shaped leaves of bold, architectural appearance, rather tropical-looking, and huge spikes of creamy white bells. The finest of all is *Y. gloriosa*, sometimes known as Adam's needle, forming a rather meandering trunk up to 1.8 m (6 ft) on top of which sits a rosette of sharply pointed leaves. *Y. recurvifolia* is similar, but the older leaves bend downwards. Both have viciously rigid, pointed tips to their leaves, quite capable of blinding anyone who inadvertently sticks a leaf in their eye when weeding, and best avoided, particularly if there are children about. The freest-flowering species is a much better bet: this is *Y. filamentosa*, a stemless, clump-forming shrub with soft recurving leaves and softer tips to the leaves; these are edged with white hanging threads. 60 cm (2 ft). Flowers to 1.2 m (4 ft), white, autumn. There is a striking variegated form. *Y. flaccida* is similar, with the leaves appearing to have been broken half-way along their length. Not quite so free in flower, but flowers earlier. A good variety is 'Ivory'. Pull off dead leaves. Increase by offsets; seed.

CHAPTER 9

CONIFERS

Conifers, especially the dwarf kinds, have an important part to play in the shrub garden, though this does not seem to have been widely appreciated until recently. They are particularly valuable for the contrast they afford with broad-leaved shrubs, both deciduous and evergreen, and many are treasured for their coloured foliage.

All those described here are evergreen, though not all conifers are evergreen. Evergreen is perhaps a misnomer, since colours vary from light green to black-green, while others are blue, gold, silver, bronze and even rosy-red. In addition to the colourfulness of their foliage they are useful, too, for their variety of shapes, ranging from the narrowly columnar Irish juniper, *Juniperus communis* 'Hibernica' to the prostrate ground-covering *Juniperus sabina tamariscifolia.*

Most can be raised from half-ripe cuttings placed in cold frame; they are, however, very slow to root and in general it is better to buy healthy plants from nurseries or garden centres. Plant in spring and protect from cold winds with a hessian screen. Water freely in their first year and keep a good mulch over the roots. Relatively free from pests and diseases.

All the conifers described here are suitable for smaller gardens.

Abies FIR
Very popular is the dwarf form of the silver fir, *Abies balsamea* 'Hudsonia', which forms a compact bun shape clothed with deep green foliage. Slow growing, to about 1 by 1.2 m (3 by 4 ft). Any soil and sun.

Cedrus CEDAR
Most of the cedars are far too large for the average garden, but not *C. deodara* 'Golden Horizon', a semi-prostrate variety, 75 cm (2½ ft) in height with a spread of 1.2 m (4 ft). That's in 10 years – ultimately it will be a bit larger. It has brilliant golden foliage all year round and makes a superb specimen plant. Needs well-drained soil and plenty of sun.

Chamaecyparis FALSE CYPRESS
There are lots of dwarf chamaecyparis to choose from. Let's start with the Lawson cypress varieties (*C. lawsoniana*). 'Ellwoodii' is popular, a compact cone of grey-green foliage, ultimately 4.5 to 6 m (15 to 20 ft) in

height. 'Ellwood's Gold' has light yellow foliage and is a much smaller plant. 'Gnome' forms a tiny deep green cone, no more than 30 cm (12 in) high in 10 years. 'Minima Aurea' is also cone shaped with bright yellow foliage, no more than 1.5 m (5 ft) in height and spread. Very slow grower, though.

A great favourite is *C. pisifera* 'Boulevard' which forms a wide cone of silvery blue foliage. Ultimately 3 m (10 ft) in height and spread. Also popular is *C. pisifera* 'Filifera Aurea' with weeping branches and golden thread-like foliage. Ultimately 3 m (10 ft) or so in height and spread. *C. thyoides* 'Ericoides' is a bun-shaped conifer whose foliage is bronze-green in summer, changing, in winter, to purple. Ultimately 1 to 1.5 m (3 to 5 ft) in height and spread. Grow all of these in any well-drained soil in an open sunny spot.

Cryptomeria JAPANESE CEDAR
C. japonica 'Vilmoriniana' is a compact bun-shaped conifer with dense, bright green foliage which turns to deep red-purple in winter. Ultimate height and spread 1 m (3 ft). Grow in sun or partial shade; needs slightly acid, well-drained yet moisture-retentive soil.

Juniperus JUNIPER
A large genus of tough, hardy plants, very variable in habit and general appearance.

Prostrate varieties *J. communis* 'Depressa Aurea', golden-yellow in summer, bronze in winter, 1.5 m (5 ft) spread in 10 years; *J. conferta*, prickly bright green foliage, spreads to 2 m (6 ft) in 10 years; *J. horizontalis* 'Bar Harbor', greyish blue foliage, 2 m (6 ft) spread in 10 years; and *J. sabina tamariscifolia*, grey-blue feathery foliage, spreads to 1 m (3 ft) in 10 years.

Taller spreading varieties *J.* × *media* 'Gold Sovereign', branches in layers, bright yellow foliage, 50 by 75 cm (20in by 2½ ft) in 10 years; *J.* × *media* 'Hetzii', layers of horizontal branches, grey-green feathery foliage, 1 by 2 m (3 by 6 ft) in 10 years; *J.* × *media* 'Pfitzerana Aurea', layers of horizontal branches, golden foliage, 75 cm by 1.5 cm (2½ by 5 ft) in 10 years; *J. squamata* 'Blue Carpet', brilliant silver-blue foliage, 30 cm by 2 m) (12 in by 6 ft) in 10 years; and *J. squamata* 'Meyeri', branches held out at an acute angle, prickly steel-blue foliage, ultimately 3 by 3 m (10 by 10 ft).

Erect varieties *J. communis* 'Compressa', a tiny grey-green cone, very slow growing – about 30 to 45 cm (12 to 18 in) high in 10 years; *J. communis* 'Hibernica', the Irish juniper, a narrow column, grey-green, ultimately up to 6 m (20 ft) high; and *J. virginiana* 'Skyrocket', a very narrow bluish grey column, ultimately at least 6 m (20 ft) in height.

Dwarf conifers come in many shades of gold, grey and green, and in varied shapes, so it is possible to create some stunning contrasts in groups of these popular plants.

The junipers grow well in any well-drained soil and are especially good on chalk. Suitable for partial shade, but golden varieties need full sun.

Picea SPRUCE

P. glauca 'Albertiana Conica' is a popular broad cone-shaped conifer with very dense bright green foliage; ultimately about 2 m (6 ft) high. *P. pungens* 'Globosa' has stunning brilliant silver-blue foliage. It's a dome-shaped plant, slow growing, ultimately attaining 1 by 1 m (3 by 3 ft). Grow spruces in open, sunny positions and any well-drained soil.

Pinus PINE

There are several dwarf pines, including *P. leucodermis* 'Compact Gem', a broad dome of deep green glossy needles, ultimately 2 by 2 m (6 by 6 ft). Then there's the dwarf mountain pine, *P. mugo*, best in its varieties 'Gnome' and 'Mops', which will only be about 60 cm (2 ft) high and wide in 10 years. All of these grow well on chalky soils, but abhor shade and industrial pollution.

Taxus YEW

There are several dwarf yews, like *T. baccata* 'Repandens', a wide-spreading shrub with deep green foliage; ultimately 50 cm high by 3 m wide (20 in by 10 ft). *T. b.* 'Summergold' is semi-prostrate with bright yellow foliage; attaining, in 10 years, a height of 50 cm and a spread of 1.2 m (20 in by 4 ft). The golden Irish yew, *T.b.* 'Fastigiata Aurea', is suitable for a small garden as it forms a narrow column. Ultimate height is about 5 m (17 ft). Yews are ideal for shady spots and chalky soil, but gold-leaved kinds give their best colour in full sun.

Thuja

One of the most popular dwarf conifers is *T. occidentalis* 'Rheingold', a broad cone of deep gold foliage, which turns to deep coppery gold in the winter. It's slow growing, in 10 years being only about 1 m high and 1.5 m wide (3 by 5 ft). Full sun needed for best colour; any well-drained soil.

CHAPTER 10

SHRUBS FOR A PURPOSE

If you have read the descriptive lists you will have noticed that certain shrubs do better in some soils and situations than in others. This can be frustrating if you do not have the right conditions for the shrub you most want to grow. On the other hand, there is another way of looking at this: ascertain what soil and conditions you have, see what will grow in those conditions and then set out to make the best combination you can. ·

The lists given here are not exhaustive, but should be helpful. Full details of all the plants mentioned here are given in the descriptive lists.

Shrubs for Autumn Colour

Acer
Azalea (deciduous)
Berberis
Cotinus
Eucryphia
Hamamelis
Rhus
Viburnum opulus

Autumn and Winter Berries

Berberis
Callicarpa
Chaenomeles
Cotoneaster
Decaisnea
Euonymus
Hippophae
Ilex
Pernettya
Pyracantha
Rosa
Skimmia
Stranvaesia
Symplocus
Viburnum

Winter Flowering Shrubs

Camellia
Chimonanthus
Cornus mas
Corylopsis
Daphne mezereum
Erica
Garrya
Hamamelis
Lonicera
Mahonia
Viburnum

Scented Shrubs

Azalea (deciduous)
Chimonanthus
Chionanthus
Choisya
Corylopsis

Daphne
Hamamelis
Lavandula
Mahonia
Osmanthus

Philadelphus
Poncirus
Rosmarinus
Syringa

Shrubs for Chalky Soils
Acer
Berberis
Buddleia
Ceanothus
Chaenomeles
Choisya
Cornus
Corylus
Cotoneaster
Daphne
Deutzia
Escallonia
Euonymus
Forsythia
Hibiscus
Ilex
Philadelphus
Potentilla
Prunus
Rhus
Ribes
Senecio
Spiraea
Syringa
Viburnum

Shrubs for Wet Ground
Cornus alba and
  vars
Corylus
Hydrangea
Salix
Viburnum opulus

Shrubs for Hot, Dry Sites
Aralia
Artemisia
Berberis
Caryopteris
Ceratostigma
Chaenomeles
Cistus
Cotoneaster (low
  growing vars)
Cytisus
Erica
Euonymus fortunei
Genista
Halimium
Hebe
Helichrysum
Hippophae
Hypericum
Juniperus
Lavandula
Perovskia
Potentilla
Rhus
Rosmarinus
Santolina
Senecio
Spartium
Spiraea
Tamarix
Vinca
Yucca

Shrubs for Shade or Partial Shade
★ = will grow
  under trees
Acer Japanese vars★
Azalea (evergreen)★
Berberis
Camellia
Chaenomeles
Choisya
Cornus alba vars
Cotoneaster (low
  growing vars★)
Daphne★
Euonymus fortunei★
Garrya
Gaultheria★
Hydrangea★
Hypericum★
Ilex – not golden
Leycesteria
Mahonia★
Pernettya★
Pieris
Pyracantha
Ribes
Rhododendron,
  some★
Sarcococca★
Skimmia★
Viburnum (winter
  flowering vars)
Vinca★

Shrubs for the Rock Garden

Acer palmatum
'Dissectum'
Azalea (evergreen)
Berberis (dwarf
vars)
Cistus

Cotoneaster (dwarf
vars)
Cytisus
Erica
Genista
Hebe

Helianthemum
Helichrysum
Lavandula
Potentilla
Santolina

APPENDIX

SELECTION OF SUPPLIERS

All of these nurseries supply catalogues and a mail–order service.

Bressingham Gardens, Bressingham, Diss, Norfolk, IP22 2AB
Hillier Nurseries (Winchester) Ltd, Ampfield House, Ampfield,
Romsey, Hampshire, SO51 9PA.
Notcutt's Nurseries Ltd, Woodbridge, Suffolk, IP12 4AF.

INDEX